Space Weapons
Earth Wars

Bob Preston | **Dana J. Johnson** | **Sean J.A. Edwards**
Michael Miller | **Calvin Shipbaugh**

D1227206

oject **AIR FORCE**

AND

epared for the United States Air Force
proved for public release; distribution unlimited

The research reported here was sponsored by the United States Air Force under Contract F49642-01-C-0003. Further information may be obtained from the Strategic Planning Division, Directorate of Plans, Hq USAF.

Library of Congress Cataloging-in-Publication Data

Space weapons : earth wars / Bob Preston ... [et al.].
   p. cm.
   "MR-1209-AF."
   Includes bibliographical references and index.
   ISBN 0-8330-2937-1
   1. Space weapons. 2. Space warfare. 3. Astronautics, Military—United States.
  4. United States—Military policy. I. Preston, Bob, 1951–

UG1530 .S72 2002
358'.8'0973—dc21

00-045926

RAND is a nonprofit institution that helps improve policy and decisionmaking through research and analysis. RAND® is a registered trademark. RAND's publications do not necessarily reflect the opinions or policies of its research sponsors.

Published 2002 by RAND
1700 Main Street, P.O. Box 2138, Santa Monica, CA 90407-2138
1200 South Hayes Street, Arlington, VA 22202-5050
201 North Craig Street, Suite 102, Pittsburgh, PA 15213-1516
RAND URL: http://www.rand.org/
To order RAND documents or to obtain additional information, contact Distribution Services: Telephone: (310) 451-7002; Fax: (310) 451-6915; Internet: order@rand.org

Since at least the era of Thomas D. White as Air Force Chief of Staff, the Air Force has espoused the full use of the medium of space for national security. Its 1997 vision document, *Global Engagement: A Vision for the 21st Century*, made clear that

> the Air Force recognizes that any further[1] use of space will be driven by national policy, international events, . . . and threats. . . . However, the nation will expect the Air Force to be prepared to defend U.S. interests in space when necessary.

Since then, the topic of full exploitation of space for national security has become prominent in current congressional interest. A national debate on space weapons seems near.

In preparation for that debate, this report is intended to provide a common vocabulary and common expectations of the possibility, utility, legalities, and limitations of using space weapons in terrestrial conflicts. This report defines and classifies these weapons, describes their different attributes, and explains how they might be used. It explores ways in which the United States and other countries could decide to acquire such weapons. It also explores the ways they could be acquired.

The study was sponsored by the Deputy Chief of Staff, Plans and Programs (AF/XP). The result should be of interest to a wide audience

---

[1] Beyond intelligence, surveillance and reconnaissance; warning; position location; weapons guidance; communications; and environmental monitoring.

interested in the military use of space and national security space policy.

Project AIR FORCE

Project AIR FORCE, a division of RAND, is the Air Force federally funded research and development center (FFRDC) for studies and analysis. It provides the Air Force with independent analyses of policy alternatives affecting the development, employment, combat readiness, and support of current and future aerospace forces. Research is performed in four programs: Aerospace Force Development; Manpower, Personnel, and Training; Resource Management; and Strategy and Doctrine.

CONTENTS

FIGURES

TABLES

SUMMARY

Space weapons for terrestrial conflict have been the subject of intense debate twice in the modern history of space. The first time, at the beginning of the Cold War, was over the possibility of bombardment satellites carrying nuclear weapons. The second time, at the end of the Cold War, was over the possibility of space-based defenses against nuclear missiles. Now, well past the Cold War, the topic of space weapons seems headed again for public debate, this time based on ballistic missile defense. National policy documents tacitly include the development of advanced technology to improve ballistic missile defense options. The latest space policy document from the Department of Defense (Cohen, 1999) supports "ballistic missile defense and force projection." To this end, the United States is developing space-based laser technology, which is approaching the demonstration phase. For these reasons, as well as the threat that space weapons could pose if developed by an adversary, it is time for public discussion of the subject.

This report does not present an argument either for or against space weapons but instead describes their attributes and sets out a common vocabulary for future discussions. The report classifies and compares these weapons and explains how they might be used. It also explores ways in which the United States and other countries might decide to acquire them and the potential reaction of other countries if the United States or some other nation fielded such weapons. The report dispels some of the myths regarding space weapons to help ensure that debates and discussions are more fact based.

SPACE WEAPONS COMPARED

It is important to understand that "space-based weapons" generally includes several distinct classes of weapons:

*   directed-energy weapons

*   kinetic-energy weapons against missile targets

*   kinetic-energy weapons against surface targets

*   space-based conventional weapons against surface targets.

Directed-energy weapons, which destroy targets with energy transmitted at the speed of light over long distances, are in a class of their own. The other three weapon types destroy targets by delivering mass to the target using either the kinetic energy of their own velocity and mass or the stored chemical energy of conventional explosives to destroy the target. Each type of weapon operates in different ways, is suitable for different kinds of targets, has different response times, and requires different numbers of weapons in orbit to achieve the degree of responsiveness required to reach a particular target when needed. Table S.1 summarizes these distinctions.

DIRECTED-ENERGY WEAPONS

Directed-energy weapons include a range of weapons from electronic jammers to laser cutting torches. While jammers need to transmit only enough power to compete with the targeted receivers' intended signals, destroying ballistic missile boosters would require developing and deploying lasers with millions of watts of power directed by optics on the order of ten meters in diameter.

Directed-energy weapons could destroy targets on or above the earth's surface, depending on the wavelength of the energy propagated and the conditions of the atmosphere, including weather. Although the energy a laser delivers propagates at the speed of light, the laser has to hold its beam on a target until energy accumulates to a destructive level at the target. After destroying a target, it can retarget as quickly as it can point at the next missile, should it have sufficient fuel. When defending against a salvo of missiles, the laser will only be able to destroy a certain number of missiles while they

Table S.1

Space Weapon Comparison

	Directed Energy	Mass-to-Target Weapons		
	Laser, radio frequency, particle beam, etc., weapons	Kinetic energy against missile targets	Kinetic energy against surface targets	Space-based conventional weapons
Targets	Soft, located from the surface to space,[a] any speed	Hardened targets above 60 km moving at great speed	Hardened fixed or slow-moving targets on earth	Hardened targets, either fixed or moving at moderate speeds, surface or air
Effects	Range from nonlethal jamming to lethal heating; finite, inherently "thin" defense	Lethal impact	Vertical, limited-depth penetrator	Inherited from conventional munitions
Responsiveness[b]	Seconds	A few minutes	A few hours	About 10 min plus time it takes weapon to reach target after delivery from space
Number of weapons in constellation	Several dozens	Several dozens for each needed to reach a particular target in desired time	About six in reserve for each needed to reach a particular target in desired time	About six in reserve for each needed to reach a particular target in desired time

[a] Depending on wavelength.
[b] Time from weapon release to target effect.

are in their vulnerable boost phase. That number will depend on the laser's distance from the launch position and the hardness of the missile target. The farther the laser weapon is based from the target and the harder the material of the target, the fewer missiles the laser will be able to destroy during boost phase. Because the distance of laser satellites from missile launch points fluctuates in a predictable way, an opponent launching missiles will be able to choose to launch at times that allow the maximum number of missiles to penetrate the defense.

Kinetic-Energy Weapons Against Missile Targets Above the Atmosphere

Kinetic-energy weapons come in two types: those designed to destroy targets outside the earth's atmosphere and those that can penetrate the earth's atmosphere. The first type, described here, could conceivably provide an additional layer of defense against targets that leak through the laser weapons' boost-phase defense. They would destroy targets using the kinetic energy of high-velocity impact and would require very little weapon mass. As with directed-energy weapons, the short response time for missile defense would require dozens of weapons in space for each one within reach of a potential target.

However, kinetic-energy weapons for use against missile targets are handicapped in their ability to respond quickly to the missile threat. They are not able to engage targets below 60 km because the interceptor needs to stay out of the atmosphere. This may mean that the intercept could only occur after the missile's boost phase, when multiple warheads and decoys may have been deployed, creating the potential for saturation an order of magnitude greater than for boost-phase defense with directed-energy weapons.

Kinetic-Energy Weapons Against Surface Targets

Space-based kinetic-energy weapons for surface targets also destroy targets by using their own mass moving at very high velocities. Unlike weapons that engage targets outside the earth's atmosphere, these must be large enough to survive reentry through the earth's atmosphere with a speed high enough to be destructive. To preserve accuracy and energy through reentry, they have to attack targets at steep, nearly vertical trajectories. This would mean having either a great many weapons in low orbits to have one within reach of a target whenever needed or a smaller number at higher orbits with longer times to reach targets. A reasonable high-altitude constellation would place about six weapons in orbit for each target to achieve response times of two to three hours from initiation of the attack to destruction of the target.

The effort required to deliver one of these weapons to orbit and then to a target would be similar to that required for a large intercontinental ballistic missile (ICBM). Such weapons could be effective against stationary (or slowly moving) surface targets that are vulnerable to vertical penetration of a few meters, such as large ships, missile silos, hardened aircraft shelters, tall buildings, fuel tanks, and munitions storage bunkers. Because of their meteoroidlike speed entering the atmosphere, these weapons would be very difficult to defend against. Although they would be of little interest to the United States because it already has weapons that are effective against this class of targets, kinetic-energy weapons could be desirable for countries that seek global power projection without having to duplicate the U.S. investment in terrestrial forces.

Space-Based Conventional Weapons Against Surface Targets

Space-based conventional weapons would inherit their accuracy, reach, target sets, and lethality from the conventional munitions they deliver. Such weapons could engage a broader range of targets than kinetic-energy weapons, including maneuvering targets and more-deeply buried targets. They could use "old" technology. The systems used to deliver them from space might resemble those developed for the return of film and biological specimens from orbit in the 1960s.

The effort to deliver conventional weapons to orbit and then to a terrestrial target is similar to that for space-based kinetic-energy weapons, but conventional weapons are much more responsive. They would take about 10 minutes from weapon release to deployment in the atmosphere, plus whatever time the conventional munitions need to reach the target after that. Small, precision weapons would be preferred for space basing, since their launch costs are higher than the costs of delivering them from aircraft or ships. It would take about six weapons in orbit to keep one within 10 minutes of a target on earth.

OVERVIEW OF CAPABILITIES

Taken together, space weapons provide a number of distinct advantages and disadvantages:

Advantages

Access and reach. Space weapons can attack targets that may be inaccessible to other weapons, could provide access to targets without concern for transit of denied airspace, and could provide global power projection to nations that possess them.

Rapid response. In contrast to weapons launched from ships or aircraft, which could take a few days to some weeks to reach a theater of operations far from the United States, space-based weapons could offer response times from several minutes to several hours. Only long-range ballistic missiles can achieve similar performance.

Distance. The great distance of space-based weapons from earth and from other objects in space has two key advantages. First, it makes space-based weapons less vulnerable to attack. Second, it would help distinguish them from terrestrial ballistic missiles carrying nuclear weapons.

Difficulty of defense. Space-based kinetic-energy weapons directed at surface targets are very difficult to defend against because of their very high velocity and very brief flight through the atmosphere. The difficulty is similar to that involved in defeating reentry vehicles from ICBMs but is complicated by the possibility of a much-shorter warning time.

Disadvantages

Static defense. Space weapons are static in the same way that stone fortifications are static; for this reason, they can be saturated by an opponent that is able to concentrate an attack against them. This limitation could be an advantage if a limited defense against a limited threat were needed, one that would be incapable of destabilizing a deterrence relationship with another more-capable opponent.

Stable, observable, predictable orbits. The positions of space-based weapons are predictable. As defenses, their effectiveness will fluctuate over the course of their orbits in predictable and exploitable ways. Stable orbits also mean that a weapon destroyed on orbit would leave a persistent cloud of debris, in a shell of nearby orbits, that would pose a hazard to other satellites.

Logistic expense. Space-based conventional or kinetic-energy weapons require greater transportation effort than do ICBMs delivering the same weapons to targets, roughly equivalent to launching the missile's payload a second time to medium range. Space-based chemical lasers that use technology now in development would consume laser reactants weighing as much as a small satellite to kill a missile target. The space-based laser weapons themselves are extremely large satellites to lift into orbit.

Large numbers required. It would generally be necessary to have multiple weapons in orbit to ensure that one of them would be in the right place when needed. Space-based ballistic missile defenses would require dozens of weapons in orbit for each needed to engage targets at a particular time and place. For other kinds of force application, constellations could be as small as three to six weapons for each needed to engage a target at a particular time and place. This is roughly comparable with terrestrial weapon platforms.

Legal consequences. Existing treaty provisions explicitly restrict the basing of missile defenses or weapons of mass destruction in space. A decision to base missile-defense weapons in space would require changing or abandoning the Anti-Ballistic Missile Treaty and related arms control treaties (as would most national missile defenses contemplated). Use of a space-based weapon against a terrestrial target could result in claims of absolute liability for damage caused under Article II of the Space Liability Convention. However, Article VI of that convention should insulate the launching state from claims of absolute liability by the targeted country if the weapon is used in legitimate self-defense.

USE AND COMMAND

One could imagine special, limited cases in which space forces could be employed in isolation from other forces, but space-based weapons would be most effective used in combination with other forces. The military functions they might serve include prompt long-range force projection, strikes against highly defended surface targets, and attacks on large ships. The one military function that directed-energy weapons would be uniquely suited for is boost-phase missile defense in locations that cannot be reached by other means.

It should be possible to develop effective concepts for the employment of space-based weapons in the context of joint warfare, but it is critical that they be integrated effectively into the command structure. A commander of theater forces having tactical control over all terrestrial assets devoted to a particular function, such as counter-air or strategic attack, should have similar control over the space assets that contribute to the mission in his area of operations.

UNDER WHAT CIRCUMSTANCES MIGHT THE UNITED STATES ACQUIRE SPACE WEAPONS?

A U.S. decision to acquire space weapons could come about under a variety of circumstances. Among them are:

- defending against a threat to national security posed by an adversary who is undeterred by other capabilities (including the case of denied-area, boost-phase missile defense)

- responding in kind to the acquisition of space weapons by another nation, whether ally or adversary

- acquiring space weapons in coordination with another nation or nations to forestall, control, or influence their independent acquisition of space weapons

- unilaterally undertaking the acquisition of space weapons on the basis of any one of several purposes, for example, to demonstrate global leadership, to protect U.S. and allied economic investments, or to improve the efficiency and effectiveness of military capability.

Although there is currently no compelling threat to U.S. national security that could not be deterred or addressed by other means, the United States could consider space-based weapons as a component of its vision of global power projection for 2010 and beyond.

WHAT MIGHT LEAD OTHER COUNTRIES TO ACQUIRE SPACE WEAPONS?

The opportunity to acquire space weapons is not limited to the United States. Only the option to acquire lethal, directed-energy weapons is proprietary to the United States, and not inherently or indefinitely, but simply as a consequence of the current state of technology.

Why would another country choose to acquire space-based weapons? The report offers answers to that question for several types of countries: peer competitors of the United States; countries that are friends or allies of the United States; non–peer competitors, neither friend nor foe; or a nonstate coalition of entities.

Although motives and opportunities may exist, there is no immediately compelling threat driving any country to choose space weapons, unless it is the overwhelming advantage in terrestrial weapons that the United States enjoys. The United States needs to be aware that a few dozen space-based kinetic-energy weapons against terrestrial targets could threaten its maritime means of power projection. The technology, numbers, and supporting space-based sensing and command and control are reasonably within reach of countries that, like India and China, have only modest spacefaring capabilities. Such space-based weapons could be a high-leverage, asymmetric response to U.S. military strengths.

Before deciding to acquire or forgo space weapons for terrestrial conflict, the United States should fully discuss what such weapons can do, what they will cost, and the likely consequences of acquiring them. The discussion should also address whether other countries might acquire them, which ones would be most likely to do so, and how the United States could discern these developments and respond effectively.

ACKNOWLEDGMENTS

This work was sponsored by Lt Gen Roger DeKok, Deputy Chief of Staff for Plans and Programs, Headquarters, USAF. The authors are indebted to General DeKok and his staff. Lt Col Forrest Morgan was the responsible action officer.

Early drafts of the manuscript benefited substantially from discussions with a number of helpful people, including Col Chuck Bauland, Col (ret) Owen "Juice" Jensen, Col (ret) Chris Waln, Col Bill Henabray, and Lt Col Douglas Anderson. The final edition owes much to critical review by Bruno Augenstein, Dean Wilkening, Burrus Carnahan, and Gen (ret) James P. McCarthy. It also owes a great deal to analysis and advice from Laura Zakaras.

ABBREVIATIONS

ABM	Anti–ballistic missile
AFSPC	Air Force Space Command
BAMBI	Ballistic Missile Boost Intercept
BMD	Ballistic missile defense
DoD	Department of Defense
ICBM	Intercontinental ballistic missile
J	joule
LOCAAS	Low Cost Autonomous Attack System
MIRV	Multiple independently targetable reentry vehicle
MRBM	Medium-range ballistic missile
OTA	Congressional Office of Technology Assessment
SDI	Strategic Defense Initiative
SDIO	Strategic Defense Initiative Organization
START	Strategic Arms Limitation Talks
UN	United Nations
Δv	Change in velocity
β	Ballistic coefficient
apogee	The point in an elliptical orbit farthest from earth and thus the highest altitude
perigee	The point in an elliptical orbit closest to the earth and thus the lowest altitude

Chapter One

INTRODUCTION

Space weapons have been debated intensely twice in the modern history of space. At the beginning of the Cold War, the issue was the possibility of bombardment satellites carrying nuclear weapons. At the end of the Cold War, the issue was the possibility of space-based defenses against nuclear missiles. Aside from these debates, there has been little public discussion of the topic. Now, well past the Cold War, the topic of space weapons is surfacing again. Military vision documents give space weapons an air of inevitability. Responsible scientific advisors to the Department of Defense (DoD) have recommended development of some space-based weapons. The official timetable for acquiring them in the next ten to twenty years implies that development decisions are imminent. A space-based laser technology program continues toward demonstration of the ability to destroy missiles from space. The current debate over national missile defense includes the issue of space-based defenses.

Regardless of the pace of the current debate, there is another, perhaps more urgent, reason to discuss space weapons: the possibility that other nations will decide to acquire them. A modest number of space-based weapons with limited space-based support could deny the United States its maritime means for power projection. Such space-based weapons, reasonably available to spacefaring countries having even the modest capabilities of India or China, could be a high-leverage, asymmetric response to U.S. military strengths.

PURPOSE

With the objective of informing the public discussion of space-based weapons, this report describes their potential attributes, limitations, legalities, and utility. It is thus a tutorial or sourcebook, not a blueprint for building such weapons or an argument for or against them. The report defines and classifies these weapons, describes their different attributes, and explains how they might be used in conflict, then explores the reasons a nation might choose to acquire them, possible means of acquiring them, and the possible consequences.

SCOPE

Since the target of this primer on space weapons in terrestrial conflict is public discussion, an unclassified discussion is essential. The critical decisionmakers in government naturally have the clearances to access any classified material they need to illuminate their own decisions. While the public does not have similar access, it is not necessary for understanding the fundamental issues well enough to hold decisionmakers accountable. Including classified material would not change the conclusions of this report. Because the examples used here are all unclassified, none of them should be taken as surrogates for real programs or proposals. The specifics of any weapon that might reveal limitations or vulnerabilities should be classified.

That the subject is space weapons in terrestrial conflict, as opposed to uses of space in conflict or weapons in space conflict, is a matter of focus. We focus on space weapons in terrestrial conflict because they are a looming decision issue. The others are not. The use of space in conflict and the use of weapons against space systems are both historical fact and current reality. From its beginning, man's use of space has included conflict, wars cold and hot: finding targets, warning of threats, relaying commands, aiding navigation, and forecasting weather. Because of this usefulness in conflict, the military use of space has long been a target. Through most of the Cold War, both sides developed, tested, and deployed weapons against satellites. Most of the world has weapons that can be used against space systems—to jam links, blind sensors, or disable ground stations. Several countries have used them, including Russia's recent jamming of communications satellites during its war in Chechnya (Agence France Press, 1999). Although weapons against space systems are not the primary focus of this report, they do come up in discussing acquisition decisions and the consequences of acquisition.

This report does not estimate costs or claim performance for specific programs or possible applications. That would require assumptions about dates, numbers, targets, and rates, as well as about competing and contributing force structures, that are beyond the scope of a tutorial. Instead, the report indicates the general scale of effort and range of attributes associated with different kinds of space-based weapons for different purposes. In some cases, it suggests relevant experience with terrestrial systems that could provide a basis for estimating costs. Both U.S. and international decisions would be made in the context of international law. Some space-based weapons are explicitly prohibited by treaty: weapons of mass destruction and, for the United States and Russia, components of ballistic missile defense. Because missile defense is one of the near-term interests driving U.S. consideration of space-based weapons, that mission is discussed here. We do not consider a U.S. decision to base weapons of mass destruction in space; there is no obvious reason the United States would want to do so. However, we do consider the possibility that another country might find reasons to do so.

ORGANIZATION

To set the stage for the tutorial material and discussion, the next chapter provides a short history of space weapons. It traces the roots of the idea in literature to the dawn of the space age, through the Cold War, and to the present. It describes the dominant perspectives toward space weapons today. Chapter Three provides brief technical descriptions of the effects, logistics, responsiveness, and basing of different kinds of space-based weapons, with more-detailed descriptions in Appendixes A, B, and C. Chapter Four builds on the "what" and "why" of the technical tutorial to explore the "so what" and "how." It examines the potential employment and command of space weapons in the broader context of other forces. Chapter Five addresses how the United States might come to a decision to acquire space weapons and how the transition from a world without space weapons to a world with U.S. space weapons might take place. Because a decision to acquire space weapons is not a purely U.S. prerogative, Chapter Six discusses who else could decide to acquire space weapons, under what circumstances, and with what kind of transition. Appendix D provides some technical background for both of these chapters, describing a low-technology class of missile-defense countermeasures that could also be used for basing a weapon of mass destruction in space. Chapter Seven provides concluding observations.

Chapter Two

BACKGROUND

One of the earliest literary traces of the idea of weapons coming from space appears in the 19th-century science fiction novel of Martian invasion by H.G. Wells, *The War of the Worlds* (Wells, 1988 ed.). Although the weapons had come from space with their extraterrestrial owners rather than being stationed there by nations of the earth, they included many of the kinds of weaponry we will see in later chapters: meteoroidlike capsules entering the earth's atmosphere from space to deliver cargoes of weapons; heat rays, which we would recognize as infrared lasers; chemical weapons; and the nemesis of the Martian invaders, biological weapons—earth's own microbes. The accuracy of his vision is impressive. It has also been durable and persuasive, as demonstrated by the public panic following Orson Welles' radio adaptation in 1938 and by the U.S. Navy's World War II intelligence assessment that the Germans could orbit satellites "for reconnaissance or for relaying what scare pieces in the press called 'death rays'" (Green and Lomask, 1997).

HISTORY

Early Rocketry

We can trace the history of the potential for real space weapons from shortly after Wells' prescient novel through the modern development of rocketry and satellites.[1] An Englishman, Charles Golightly, had

---

[1]Unless noted otherwise, the timing of the historical events cited in the material below is documented in Emme (1961).

registered a patent for a rocket-powered vehicle as early as 1841 (Noordung, 1929). Rigorous theoretical discussion of rocket propulsion for spaceflight was pursued as early as 1903 by Konstantin Tsiolkolvskiy in Russia (Green and Lomask, 1997) and later by Robert Goddard in the United States (1919) and Hermann Oberth in Germany (1923) (Noordung, 1929). In 1924, the Soviet Union formed the Central Committee for the Study of Rocket Propulsion. In the Kitty Hawk event of rocketry, Goddard launched the first modern, liquid-fueled rocket in 1926. Technical and amateur societies for spaceflight were established in Germany (1927), France (1927), and the United States (1930). In August 1932, the German Army Ordnance Office established a military rocket development program, which resulted eventually in the development of the V-2 ballistic missile, first tested on June 13, 1942. By the end of World War II, some 2,800 V-2s had been fired at targets in England and on the Continent.

Coincident with the development of the V-2 in Germany was that of the atomic bomb in the United States. The first controlled atomic chain reaction occurred in Chicago on December 2, 1942. The first use of the atomic bomb in war followed on August 6, 1945. The coincidence of nuclear weapons and modern rocketry provided a synergistic reinforcement of incentives for rapid development of missiles, weapons, and satellites. A push followed to make the weapons small enough to fit on missiles, which could reach further and faster than aircraft and could bypass air defenses. The weapons' enormous destructive power made missiles, which were previously of marginal military value, potentially decisive weapons. And extending the missiles' reach incidentally made them suitable for placing satellites in orbit. Satellites became the essential platforms for discerning the threat that weapons based in the interior regions of closed societies posed. The destructive power of nuclear weapons and the immediate reach of long-range missiles formed the backdrop for public attitudes about space vehicles and space weapons. That backdrop persists today in popular views of space weapons, linked explicitly with nuclear weapons in ballistic missile defense.

Satellite Feasibility Studies

In January 1945, Germany tested a prototype of a missile with an intercontinental range that could have reached the United States. By

October of that year, the U.S. Navy Bureau of Aeronautics established a Committee for Evaluating the Feasibility of Space Rocketry. In November, the committee recommended a high priority for satellite development and optimistically estimated the cost of developing one at between $5 million and $8 million. When the Navy approached the Army Air Force to discuss a joint program, General Curt LeMay, then the Deputy Chief of Staff for Research and Development, commissioned the Douglas Aircraft Corporation's Project RAND to produce a quick assessment of satellite feasibility in time for discussions with the Navy. The seminal RAND report, *Preliminary Design of an Experimental World-Circling Spaceship*, developed the technical basis for a small (500 lb, 20 ft³), low-altitude (300 mi), experimental satellite and projected the cost to develop one a little more conservatively, at about $150 million over five years (Clauser et al., 1946).

The RAND report included a short section on potential uses of satellites. Among the military uses listed were reconnaissance, weather observation, communications relay, missile guidance, bomb impact spotting, and weapons: "after observation of its trajectory, a control impulse can be applied in such direction and amount, and at such a time, that the satellite is brought down on its target" (Clausen et al., 1946, p. 10). The RAND report also predicted that "the achievement of a satellite craft by the United States would inflame the imagination of mankind, and would probably produce repercussions in the world comparable to the explosion of the atomic bomb" (Clausen et al., 1946, p. 2). Another RAND report the next year turned that observation around:

> one can imagine the consternation and admiration that would be felt here if the United States were to discover that some other nation had already put up a successful satellite.[2]

This observation was as prescient of Sputnik as Wells had been of exotic weapons.

---

[2]James Lipp, "The Time Factor in the Satellite Program," in *Reference Papers Relating to a Satellite Study*, RAND RA-15032, 1947 (quoted in Davies and Harris, 1988, p. 17).

Dawn of the Space Age

Despite the military service interest in satellites at the time of those early studies, U.S. public, international, and even senior DoD attitudes toward the military interest ranged from skepticism (of feasibility or utility) and ridicule to outrage and fear. Disclosure of the services' study activity in the first annual report of the Secretary of Defense in 1948 provoked such responses from journalists as "Will America possess moons of war?" and "Will the Elbe frontier be defended from the moon?" and "a campaign calculated to terrorize the people" (Air War College Evaluation Staff, 1956, p. 31). In congressional testimony in 1945, Dr. Vannevar Bush, by 1948 chairman of the DoD's Research and Development Board, was derisively skeptical of the feasibility of even long-range missiles, much less satellites (Peebles, 1997, pp. 4–7). It should come as no surprise that the board's March 1948 evaluation of service satellite proposals was that

> neither the Navy nor the USAF has as yet established either a military or a scientific utility commensurate with the presently expected cost of a satellite vehicle. However, the question of utility deserves further study and examination. (Emme, 1961.)

Further study focused first on reconnaissance from space. RAND's Project Feedback studies in 1953 and 1954 produced preliminary designs of weather and photographic reconnaissance satellites, which resulted in formal Air Force requirements and program direction to begin developing a reconnaissance satellite in 1954 and 1955. With growing concern over the possibility of a Soviet surprise attack, President Dwight Eisenhower commissioned scientific leaders to advise him of means to avoid surprise. The euphemistically named Technological Capabilities Panel produced a final report, *Meeting the Threat of Surprise Attack*, on Valentine's Day 1955. Among other things, the report recommended a satellite program to establish a legal precedent for the freedom of space for eventual reconnaissance satellites. That recommendation produced the National Science Foundation proposal for flying a satellite as part of the International Geophysical Year and, subsequently, a delay of the fabrication of a reconnaissance satellite until after the civil pathfinder (Peebles, 1997, pp. 15–25). The policy to use a civil precedent setter before inviting a military response to a military space launch went so far as a gag order forbidding General Bernard Schriever, the Air Force pioneer of missile and space development, to use the word *space* in public speeches when he proposed that the United States should establish space superiority in February 1957 (Futrell, 1989, pp. 549–550; Peebles, 1997, p. 26).

All that changed on October 4, 1957, when the Soviets launched Sputnik, and the U.S. public, press, and political opposition reacted with shock. By November 29, the Air Force Chief of Staff could say in his "dawn of the space age" speech that

> We airmen who have fought to assure that the United States has the capability to control the air are determined that the United States must win the capability to control space. (Futrell, 1989, p. 550.)

By December 5, President Eisenhower had directed the Corona program to develop reconnaissance satellites covertly. By August 1960, the United States had flown its first photographic reconnaissance, weather, navigation, signals intelligence, missile warning, and communications satellites—first articles of all of the current U.S. military space activities—seven months before the first human made it to orbit (AFA, 1998; Hall, 1998). The comprehensiveness and preponderance of military firsts reflect Eisenhower's judgment that

> the highest priority should go of course to space research with a military application, but because national morale, and to some extent national prestige, could be affected by the results of peaceful space research, this should likewise be pushed, but through a separate agency. (Eisenhower, 1965.)

Bombardment Satellites

Weapons were not left out of discussions of the many military applications of space explored in the post-Sputnik rush. Only 12 days after Sputnik's launch, the Air Force fired a blast of pellets into orbital and escape velocities from an Aerobee sounding rocket, although this was not intended as a weapon (Emme, 1961).[3] In 1956, the Air

---

[3]Only the pellets with earth escape velocity would have persisted for long in space. Since the Aerobee's highest altitude was only 54 miles, this would be the lowest altitude for pellets reaching orbital velocity. At this altitude, orbits would quickly decay, and the pellets would reenter the atmosphere.

Force's Air University evaluation staff, in proposing legal regimes for outer space, considered bombardment from satellites to have significant advantages over ballistic missiles. In fact, the Soviets apparently considered the perceived advantages real enough to develop and test such a system in the next decade (Air War College Evaluation Staff, 1956, p. 26). President Eisenhower's science advisors, on the other hand, judged space to be an unsuitable arena for weapons, labeling space weapons "clumsy and ineffective ways of doing a job" (Killian, 1977, p. 297) in their 1958 catalog of uses of space. We will explore the issues behind both points of view in greater detail in Chapter Three.

A Space Policy Subcommittee of the National Security Council summarized U.S. space development programs in a then-Secret document in June 1958. In the 1950s, well before the Outer Space Treaty of 1967, the Eisenhower administration sponsored development programs for anti–intercontinental ballistic missiles (ICBMs), early warning missile detection satellites, reconnaissance satellites, military communications satellites, satellites for electronic countermeasures (jamming), navigation satellites, "manned defensive outer space vehicles (which might capture, destroy, or neutralize an enemy [sic] outer space vehicles)," bombardment satellites, and a manned lunar station (National Security Council, 1958).

To develop an understanding of the possibilities for and limitations of using constellations of bombardment satellites as delivery platforms for nuclear weapons, RAND studied them in some detail from 1958 through 1960. Meanwhile, the United States carried on a public debate about orbital bombardment systems:

> Week after week during 1960 the US aerospace trade journals paraded out another orbital weapon system, designed either to attack the Soviet Union and her artificial satellites or to nullify her limited ICBMs. (Johnson, 1987b, p. 31.)

An outline of this policy debate can be found in Schelling (1963). He discussed nuclear bombardment satellites as weapon systems (including issues of accuracy, reliability, timing, costs, ability to penetrate defenses, recoverability, control, and relationship to other weapon systems) to predict the motivations for wanting them, the uses they might be put to, and the implications for the balance of military force, concepts of war, and arms control. Schelling predicted that military activity in space would become acceptable for communication, weather observation, reconnaissance, and mapping (all of which had already begun, with little public fanfare or debate) and suggested that nuclear bombardment satellites might constitute a separable class of military object that could be agreed to be unacceptable in space, if only as a clear statement of commitment to the idea of arms control.

The studies and debate on bombardment satellites were conducted against a backdrop of international negotiations to restrict the placement of nuclear weapons in space. On October 17, 1963, the negotiations culminated in United Nations (UN) General Assembly Resolution 1884 (XVIII), which called on states

> to refrain from placing in orbit around the earth any objects carrying nuclear weapons or any other kinds of weapons of mass destruction or from installing such weapons on celestial bodies.

The resolution was formalized in the 1967 Treaty on Principles Governing the Activities of States in the Exploration and Use of Outer Space, including the Moon and Other Celestial Bodies (UN, 1967).

Despite the resolution and treaty, the Soviets tested a fractional orbit bombardment system in 1966 and 1967 (Johnson, 1987b, p. 131; Stares, 1985, pp. 92, 99–100). There had been public statements suggesting the ability as early as 1962 and public displays of a purported system in 1965. In contrast to a ballistic missile, which puts its weapon payload into a ballistic trajectory that will intersect the earth without further maneuvering, a fractional orbit bombardment system injects its payload into a satellite orbit that continues around the earth if not maneuvered into another (deorbit) trajectory that intersects the earth.

The primary perceived advantage of a fractional orbit bombardment system was a shorter time of visibility to defense sensors in the target area because the orbital portion of its trajectory (around 160 km) was lower than that of a ballistic missile's trajectory (which would normally reach a peak altitude of about 1,300 km) (Garwin and Bethe, 1968, p. 26). Fractional orbit bombardment weapons could also approach their intended targets from any direction, even from the south, making them invisible to the U.S. early warning sensors of the time. However, the attacker paid a price for complicating the defender's surveillance and warning problem: payload had to decrease substantially to make way for the additional fuel needed for achieving orbit and the subsequent deorbit maneuver. Also, with the guidance and navigation capabilities of the time, the orbital bombardment system would have been less accurate than ballistic missiles (Johnson, 1987b, p. 132). Chapter Three will quantify the "price" of orbital bombardment in terms of the extra effort relative to ballistic missiles.

Two other developments also made fractional orbit bombardment less interesting. Space-based missile-warning sensors could detect and warn defenders of impending bombardment independently of trajectory altitude. The arrival of submarine-based ballistic missiles presented a more effective alternative to fractional orbit bombardment, complicated defenses, and assured a survivable deterrent force.[4] The price of fractional orbit bombardment was not worth the limited advantage to be gained.

Defenses

The specter of bombardment satellites and the reality of ballistic missiles stimulated both the United States and the Soviet Union to explore defensive space weapons. The Soviet Union first tested the *Polyot* interceptor in 1963 and successfully tested a coorbital antisatellite (ASAT) weapon in 1968 (Peebles, 1997, p. 241). In 1954, a RAND researcher described a concept for a large (approximately 1,000 vehicles), low-altitude (250–300 mi. altitude) constellation of satellites to intercept ballistic missiles early in their flights with costs comparable to air defenses of the time (Raymond, 1954). The United States tested air-launched ballistic missiles as ASAT weapons in 1959 (Air Force) and again in 1962 (Navy). A program called Ballistic Missile Boost Intercept (BAMBI) studied space-based, conventionally armed ballistic missile interceptors in some detail in the

---

[4]The missiles were smaller, and an arguably greater logistic infrastructure was necessary to maintain them on station.

early 1960s, but the concept was discarded (Flax, 1986, p. 49).[5] The United States eventually deployed an operational ground-based, nuclear-armed, ASAT missile in 1964 (Stares, 1985, pp. 108–128).

ABM Treaty

Through the 1950s and 1960s, both the United States and the Soviet Union developed land-based, nuclear-armed missiles to defend against ICBMs. The Soviet Union deployed a defense around Moscow. The U.S. defense was intended to preserve some portion of its land-based ICBMs. In the United States, funding and deployment of the defense was contentious, primarily because of concern about the defense's contribution to a continuing arms race (Nitze, 1985). In the end, both sides agreed to limit anti–ballistic missile (ABM) defenses as part of their framework of arms control treaties. The United States abandoned deployment of its land-based defense, choosing to rely instead on deterrence.

Adopted in 1972 as part of the first round of Strategic Arms Limitation Talks (SALT I), with the Soviet Union, the ABM Treaty contains specific limitations on space weapons for missile defense. The terms of the treaty prohibit the signatories from undertaking efforts

> to develop, test, or deploy new ABM systems or components which are sea-based, air-based, *space-based*, or mobile land-based. (Article V[1]; emphasis added.)

ABM systems are those that "counter strategic ballistic missiles or their elements in flight trajectory." The *components* are ABM interceptor missiles, launchers, and radars (Article II). Systems and components cannot be tested "in an ABM mode," that is, against strategic ballistic missiles or their elements in flight trajectory. The treaty also prohibits non-ABM component testing "in an ABM mode" (Article VI). Recognizing the potential of future advanced technologies, Agreed Statement D of the treaty also subjects ABM systems and components based on other physical principles to discussion.

---

[5]Until revived in the SDI era, first as a space-based interceptor and later as Brilliant Pebbles.

The Strategic Defense Initiative

Research and studies of ballistic missile defense continued throughout the Cold War, including space-based weapons. During the Reagan administration in the 1980s, vigorous public debate surfaced with the Strategic Defense Initiative (SDI), a sustained, significant investment in technologies for defense against ballistic missiles.[6] The initiative explored space-based defenses—interceptors, directed-energy weapons,[7] and even nuclear weapons (x-ray lasers). All these space-based missile defenses would require renegotiation or abrogation of the ABM Treaty and presumably also of related arms control treaties. The last item would also violate the Outer Space Treaty's ban on nuclear weapons in space.[8]

According to a Ballistic Missile Defense Organization historian, the threat of space weapons in terrestrial conflict was one factor in advice supporting President Ronald Reagan's decision to reinvigorate investment in ballistic missile defense, which previous administrations had discarded and which the 1972 ABM Treaty with the Soviet Union limited. The threat of space weapons this time was not from nuclear weapons on bombardment satellites, but from space-based directed-energy weapons. Karl Bendetson and the High Frontier panel of private citizens advising Reagan recommended a crash program to develop missile defenses not just to defend against Soviet nuclear weapons but also because of "strong indications" that the Soviets were going to deploy "powerful directed energy weapons" in space to gain control of space, which, they alleged, would "alter the balance of world power" (Baucom, 1995, pp. 190, 193). To avoid this,

---

[6]For SDI-era surveys of space weapons issues, see Long, Hafner, and Boutwell (1986) and Nye et al. (1987). For a thorough history of the SDI Organization (SDIO), see FitzGerald (1994).

[7]Directed-energy weapons include lasers, high-energy particle beams, and high-power microwave beams.

[8]To avoid the issue of nuclear weapons in space, proponents of the x-ray laser offered to base it on the earth or in the oceans on missiles that would lift the weapon above the atmosphere where its x-rays could propagate to the target. The resulting race to catch up with its target missiles before they proliferated aimpoints by releasing decoys and submunitions would have made for a challenging operational concept. In any case, developing the technology for the weapon turned out to be more difficult than proponents anticipated (FitzGerald, 2000, p. 374). Development now would be problematic with the Comprehensive Test Ban Treaty (Department of State, 2000). We will not explore this weapon further in subsequent chapters.

High Frontier's memorandum urged corresponding U.S. development of space-based directed-energy weapons and other missile defenses.[9]

With the end of the Cold War, the focus of U.S. ballistic missile defense research shifted from strategic to theater defenses and largely away from space-based weapons.

POST–COLD WAR

The idea of space weapons for terrestrial conflict has survived the Cold War in national policy. However, current policy and plans treat the idea as a future issue.

Current U.S. Policy and Plans

The U.S. national space policy includes explicit goals for strengthening and maintaining national security and promoting international cooperation to further U.S. national security and foreign policy.[10] The national space policy directs the conduct of specific space activities necessary for national defense, with emphasis on activities that support military operations worldwide, monitor and respond to threats, and monitor arms control and nonproliferation agreements and activities. The language suggests that the emphasis is on support but does not specifically preclude the possibility of space weapons. The generic catch-all is of providing support for the inherent right of self-defense with the following, more specific, details (the White House, 1996):

- Deter; warn; and, if necessary, defend against enemy attack.

- Ensure that hostile forces cannot prevent U.S. use of space.

- If necessary, counter the hostile use of space.

- Maintain the capability to execute mission areas of space control and force application.

---

[9] For more complete discussions of the policy debate over these weapons in the Cold War context, see Durch (1984), Gray (1982), and Payne (1983).

[10] The national policy was updated in 1996, after having last been published in 1989.

• Consistent with treaty obligations, develop, operate, and maintain space-control capabilities to ensure freedom of action for the United States and to deny freedom of action to U.S. adversaries.

• Pursue a ballistic missile defense program to enhance theater missile defenses, to provide readiness for national missile defense as a hedge against emergence of a long-range threat, and to develop advanced technology options to improve planned and deployed defenses.

Defense against enemy attack, counters to the hostile use of space, and ballistic missile defense may all be attempted with terrestrial or atmospheric weapons. Administration exercise of the line-item veto in 1997 explicitly singled out congressionally added space-based ballistic missile defense and ASAT development programs for veto in favor of terrestrial weapons. On missile defense, administration spokesmen said:

> Our own development program within the Department of Defense for a possible national missile defense deployment option . . . does not include space-based weapons in its architecture. (Raines, Bell, and Hamre, 1997.)

On ASAT weapons, the administration position was:

> We simply do not believe that this ASAT capability is required, at least based on the threat as it now exists and is projected to evolve over the next decade or two . . . we are confident that alternatives exist . . . including destroying ground stations linked to the satellite or jamming the links themselves. (Raines, Bell, and Hamre, 1997.)

Space force application sounds like space weapons in the national space policy's direction to maintain a capability for that mission area, but Air Force Space Command's (AFSPC's) discussion of the mission area in its mission statement refers only to terrestrially based ICBMs (AFSPC, 1998). The national policy does not rule out space weapons implicitly in its commitment to develop advanced technology to improve planned ballistic missile defense options.

The DoD updated its own space policy in 1999 (Cohen, 1999) to incorporate the new national space policy and recognize changes in technology, international environment, resources, force structure, and the commercial space industry.[11] The memorandum transmitting the new policy referred to the capability to control space with the caveat "if directed" and to the ability to perform space force application as a possibility "in the future." DoD directive 3100.10 defined force application more generally than it did ballistic missiles, as

> Combat operations in, through, and from space to influence the course and outcome of conflict. The force application mission area includes: BMD and force projection (Cohen, 1999, p. 9).

The policy directed long-range planning to "provide space control capabilities consistent with Presidential policy as well as U.S. and applicable international law." It directed long-range planning to "explore force application concepts, doctrine, and technologies" subject to the same constraints (Cohen, 1999, p. 9).

The plan that documents U.S. Space Command's roadmap to its vision of the future acknowledges that the "notion of weapons in space is not consistent with national policy" but provides "alternatives to civilian leaders if a decision is made that this capability is in the national interest" (Estes, 1998, Ch. 6). Among the alternatives described for missile defense are space-based lasers, high-power microwave weapons, and interceptors. For terrestrial targets, it lists space-based lasers, high-power microwaves, and a maneuverable reentry vehicle to dispense precision conventional munitions. The Defense Science Board has recommended some space weapons—specifically, space-based kinetic energy weapons for terrestrial targets and space-based lasers for missile defense—for joint operations in 2010 and beyond (Bender, 1999). The Space Command's long-range plan calls for policymakers to "shape [the] international community to accept space-based weapons to defend against threats in accordance with national policy" (Estes, 1998, p. 139).

LEGAL CONSIDERATIONS

Because one of the uses of space weapons of current interest to the United States is explicitly illegal, a brief survey of law applicable to

---

[11]The DoD policy had last been published in 1987.

space weapons, which is an intersection of international law and the laws of spacefaring nation-states, is appropriate. This section will survey existing space treaties and laws to identify those with particular relevance to space weapons.[12]

The United States is a party to a number of treaties and international agreements that either pertain directly to space operations (e.g., the Outer Space Treaty) or possess relevant environmental, arms control, or system constraints that include space (e.g., the ABM Treaty) or that may possibly affect or influence space operations (e.g., the Environmental Modification Convention).

Space Treaties

Efforts in the late 1950s and early 1960s to confine the use of space to peaceful purposes led to the Treaty on Principles Governing the Activities of States in the Exploration and Use of Outer Space, Including the Moon and Other Celestial Bodies, more commonly known as the Outer Space Treaty. This treaty provides the basis for further elaboration of specific points in subsequent treaties, among them the Astronaut Rescue Agreement (1968), the Space Liability Convention (1972), and the Convention on the Registration of Space Objects (1975). The Outer Space Treaty prohibits placing "objects carrying nuclear weapons or any other kinds of weapons of mass destruction" in orbit or on celestial bodies (Article IV). Activities on the moon and other celestial bodies will be for peaceful purposes only, and

> the establishment of military bases, installations and fortifications, the testing of any type of weapons and the conduct of military maneuvers on celestial bodies shall be forbidden (Article IV).

International cooperation is strongly emphasized, including launching states offering other states the opportunity to observe the flight of space objects (Article X), providing appropriate information about space activities to the Secretary-General of the UN (Article XI), and honoring requests to visit space installations on the basis of reciprocity (Article XII).

---

[12]Much of this section has been derived and updated from Johnson (1987). Another major source is ACDA (1990).

Several treaties were later built on the principles expressed in the Outer Space Treaty and are further elaborations of its Articles V, XII, X, and XI:

- the Agreement on the Rescue of Astronauts, the Return of Astronauts, and the Return of Objects Launched into Outer Space, also known as the Astronaut Rescue Agreement (1968)

- the Convention on International Liability for Damage Caused by Space Objects, also known as the Space Liability Convention (1972)

- the Convention on the Registration of Objects Launched into Outer Space (1975).

The Astronaut Rescue Agreement focuses on rendering assistance to astronauts in distress. Its relevance to space weapons lies in the provisions for recovery and return of space objects to the responsible "launching authority" (state or international organization).

The Space Liability Convention assigns responsibility to the launching state for damage caused to another state by a space object and establishes procedures for filing claims for compensation. Article II of the treaty assigns absolute liability for damage caused on the earth or in the atmosphere by a space object to the launching state. Article III assigns liability for damage caused in space to the launching state if it is negligent. Article II's absolute liability could be the basis for claims against a state that launched weapons into space for any damage those weapons cause on earth or in the atmosphere. However, Article VI exonerates the launching state from absolute liability for damage that "resulted either wholly or partially from gross negligence or from an act or omission done with intent to cause damage on the part of a claimant State." Acts done with intent to cause damage on the part of a claimant state would seem to include acts for which a launching state could reasonably claim the right of self-defense in use of a space-based weapon. On that basis, the weapon launching state might go beyond asserting exoneration from absolute liability and claim reparations for the claimant state's belligerent acts. At worst, the launching state might claim reparations offsetting its liability for using the weapon. Alternatively, a state acquiring space weapons could choose to withdraw from the convention with a year's notice.

The Convention on the Registration of Objects Launched into Outer Space establishes a central register of space objects in the UN, to which launching states are to furnish the following information "as soon as practicable" (Article IV):

1. the name of the launching state(s)

2. the space object designator or its registration number

3. the date and location of launch

4. orbital parameters, including nodal period, inclination, apogee, and perigee

5. the general function of the space object.

Furthermore, each state is required to notify the U.N. Secretary General, "to the greatest extent feasible and as soon as practicable," of space objects no longer in orbit (Article V). This treaty could complicate hiding space weapons on orbit.

Arms Control Treaties

The treaty of most direct relevance is the ABM Treaty. However, any weapon that would raise issues with this treaty would also raise issues with all the strategic arms control and nonproliferation agreements limiting nuclear weapons that are tied to it. The treaty was negotiated in the belief that ballistic missile defense could be readily overcome by proliferating offensive systems. Therefore, since deploying ABM systems might encourage the proliferation of offensive forces, limiting development and deployment of ABM systems would in turn encourage limitation of strategic offensive nuclear forces (Nitze, 1985). The treaty has received renewed attention in recent years, both during the SDI's exploration of missile defenses and, more recently, in renewed discussions with Russia over the possibility of deploying theater missile defenses and a limited national missile defense.

The terms of the treaty prohibit the two signatories from undertaking efforts "to develop, test, or deploy new ABM systems or components which are sea-based, air-based, space-based, or mobile land-based" (Article V[1]). Article II defines *systems* in terms of their ability "to counter strategic ballistic missiles or their elements in flight trajectory" and *components* as ABM interceptor missiles, launchers, and radars. Systems and components cannot be tested "in an ABM mode," that is, against strategic ballistic missiles or their elements in flight trajectory. The treaty also prohibits non-ABM component testing "in an ABM mode" (Article II). Recognizing the potential of future advanced technologies, Agreed Statement D of the ABM Treaty states:

> [I]n order to ensure fulfillment of the obligation not to deploy ABM systems and their components except as provided in Article III of the Treaty, the Parties agree that in the event ABM systems based on other physical principles and including components capable of substituting for ABM interceptor missiles, ABM launchers, or ABM radars are created in the future, specific limitations on such systems and their components would be subject to discussion in accordance with Article XIII and agreement in accordance with Article XIV of the Treaty.

At five-year intervals, the Standing Consultative Commission reviews the ABM Treaty in accordance with the provisions of Article XIV. Recently, the Clinton administration has held discussions with the Yeltsin and Putin governments in Russia concerning theater and national ballistic missile defense. A Department of State fact sheet summarizes the consequences of these discussions for space-based components of ballistic missile defense:

> The Parties also agreed not to develop, test, or deploy space-based TMD interceptor missiles or space-based components based on other physical principles (OPP) such as lasers that are capable of substituting for space-based TMD interceptor missiles. . . . As a practical matter, distinguishing space-based ABM interceptor missiles from space-based TMD interceptor missiles is difficult if not impossible. Similar difficulties arise in distinguishing between space-based components based on OPP capable of substituting for ABM interceptor missiles and space-based components based on OPP capable of substituting for TMD interceptor missiles. (Department of State, 1997.)

Other Treaties

A number of other treaties and international agreements could influence the acquisition and development of space weapons, including the Convention on the Prohibition of Military or Any Other Hostile Use of Environmental Modification Techniques (commonly known as the Environmental Modification Convention) and such others as The Hague Convention on the laws of war.[13] These treaties and agreements contain provisions that could influence system and weapon design, operation, and content. For example, environmental modification could include attempts to create an orbital debris field or enhanced radiation belts to harm satellites.

---

[13]Convention with Respect to the Laws and Customs of War on Land, with Annex of Regulations (signed at The Hague, July 29, 1899; entered into force April 9, 1902; replaced by Convention of October 18, 1907, as between contracting parties to the later convention). 32 Stat. 1803; TS 403; 36 Stat. 2277; TS 539.

Chapter Three

KINDS AND CAPABILITIES OF SPACE WEAPONS

By space weapons, we mean things intended to cause harm that are based in space or that have an essential element based in space. The degree of harm we include in defining space weapons may range from temporary disruption to permanent destruction or death. This definition does not include things that are based on the earth and transit space without achieving orbit, such as ballistic missiles. Although the dynamics are similar, the logi.more important, the legal regimes are different for the two types of weapons.

We also do not mean things in spr," not mature.estrial weapons, such as reconnaissance, navigation, weather or communications satellites. The improvements such satellites provide certainly make some of them targets themselves in terrestrial conflict. And while some of the space weapons we consider may also be useful against targets in space, our interest here is in war on earth rather than war in space. As Chapter Two pointed out, weapons against targets in space are old news, and all of them developed to date have been based on earth, not in space. We also do not mean information weapons that might use space-based communications for access to the database, decisionmaker, or computer that is their target.

TYPES OF SPACE WEAPONS

Space weapons are not all alike. They differ importantly in the physical principles they use, in the physical constraints that limit them, and in the targets they can attack. This chapter will characterize space weapons in a technical way—what they might look like, how they would work, what kinds of targets they could attack, how they scale, what their logistic issues are, and how they would compare to more-familiar weapons. The discussion includes general issues of the costs of owning space-based weapons, in particular, the circumstances and performance regimes in which the costs might be comparable to those of terrestrial alternatives. It also suggests reference points from which more specific cost projections could be made. However, more-detailed costing requires decisions on numbers of weapons and specific targets, as well as assumptions about the operational concept and context, including other competing and contributing force structure elements. This level of detail is beyond our scope here.

We will divide the discussion into two general types of weapons: (1) those that direct destructive energy to their targets without transporting significant mass and (2) those that must deliver significant mass to their targets for destructive effect. Within the second category, we will differentiate between weapons that rely on the kinetic energy of their own mass and velocity for destructive effect and those that deliver a more-conventional warhead with stored chemical energy for destructive effect.

DIRECTED-ENERGY WEAPONS

General Characteristics

The most significant characteristic of this class of weapon is propagation of destructive energy at very high speeds. Space basing of directed-energy weapons (or of the means to direct a terrestrial weapon's energy to target) seems a natural match for the long distances from space to targets on earth. For some fleeting targets and denied-area locations, there might be no other way to have any destructive energy available in time. Early posters for space-based lasers in missile defense used the catch phrase "defense at the speed of light."

However, while the speed of propagation may be dazzling, the speed of effect will be more pedestrian. Because useful effects take time to accumulate or sustain and time to redirect from target to target, the capacity of directed-energy weapons is inherently limited. The specific limits depend on the scale and duration of effect necessary for the military purpose at hand. Useful levels of disruptive or destructive energy at the target range from gentle to extreme; the class of weapons we discuss here includes the range from electronic jammers to laser cutting torches. At the level of jamming, a weapon consists of a radio transmitter tuned to cover a target range of frequencies and focused on target receivers to achieve a power level high enough to compete with the receivers' intended signals. At the level of destruction, a weapon supplies enough power to heat some critical component of the target beyond its ability to survive.

The challenge in achieving destructive levels of directed energy from space is scaling up to the power levels and component sizes needed to focus a lethal energy level over the much greater distances inherent in space basing. For example, a laser welding machine in a factory typically uses a laser with a few hundred to a few thousand watts of power directed by optics with a diameter less than 0.1 m. A space-based laser intended for targets on or near the earth requires millions of watts of power and optics with a diameter of about 10 m. The ability to create effects at the level of interference or disruption (e.g., jamming) is readily available worldwide; generating and directing the more destructive effects from or through space is a stretch for everyone.

While both generating and directing destructive levels of energy may be challenging, the technology for directing energy will have the greatest leverage for basing the weapons in space. The critical technologies are large, deployable optics for lasers and large, deployable antennas for radio frequency weapons. The technologies for both will mature and diffuse at some rate for science and surveillance—independently of weapons development.

When the technologies do mature, space-based directed-energy weapons could have the potential to engage targets from the surface of the earth outwards, depending on the form of the directed-energy selected. Their targets will generally have to be relatively soft, such as aircraft and missiles (not armored vehicles), but may be very swift. The weapons' effects may range from temporary interference to permanent destruction and should be available within seconds of release authority. Even so, the cumulative effects available against multiple targets in any window of time will be bounded by the finite time needed for the desired effect against an individual target.

Weapons capable of destructive effects will be large and expensive. For example, a single space-based laser for missile defense would be something like the combination of a next-generation space telescope with a large rocket engine and its propellant tanks. The combination is challenging because the telescope is a precision instrument requiring precise, stable pointing despite being subjected to the noise and vibration of a large rocket engine firing. Some technologies would have the additional challenges of highly corrosive fuel and exhaust from the laser.

Space-based directed-energy weapons cannot provide leak-proof defenses. As with all space-based defenses, these weapons are inherently static and subject to saturation. Because their effectiveness falls off with the square of the range to the target,[1] they will likely have lower orbits—in easier reach of terrestrial weapons. Such orbits also mean that the absentee ratios for engaging time-critical targets on or near the earth will be in the dozens.[2]

Variation of effectiveness with range also means that there is a predictable fluctuation over time in the capacity of a constellation of weapons to engage urgent targets. Weapon sizes and basing altitudes can be used to control the magnitude and shape of that fluctuation. The fluctuation in capacity creates a reserve that may be used against less-urgent targets, if consumables are replenished in time.

The remainder of this section briefly explains and illustrates these characteristics of space-based directed-energy weapons. A more-detailed explanation is available in Appendix A.

Targets

The essence of logistics is knowing how much is enough and what it takes to deliver that much where and when needed. Understanding

---

[1] Or, conversely, their size grows with the square of the range needed.

[2] The *absentee ratio* is the number of platforms needed to have one in place when needed. For satellites, the absentee platforms are in other orbital positions waiting for the combination of earth's rotation and orbital motion to bring them within reach.

the quantity and timing of effort required begins with selecting targets and effects to achieve a desired objective. Understanding how much energy is enough per target begins with determining the effect desired on or in the target.

The amount of energy needed *at* the target to produce the desired effect depends on how the weapon's energy couples with the target. Factors that influence the degree or efficiency of coupling include the target's materials, configuration, and orientation and how these interact with the particular characteristics of the energy the weapon transmits. Laser energy interacts with the surface of the target. High-energy particles penetrate further into the target. To protect the target, it helps to have materials that do not absorb a weapon's energy efficiently, as well as a shape and an orientation that minimize exposure to the harmful energy. These preferences may directly conflict with the target's purpose, particularly if it relies on energy in a similar form for its own function, for example, sensing or communication. The weapon's budget for energy needed at the target must include an assumption about the efficiency of coupling (or, equivalently, of the hardness of the target) and some degree of uncertainty about the assumption. For the more-subtle effects, it will be necessary to have feedback to confirm effectiveness despite the uncertainty.

For a representative instance of the magnitude and range of target hardness, ballistic missile boosters could be destroyed by burning a hole through a propellant tank by depositing something like about 1 to 30 kJ of energy of energy per cm^2 of target spot area, depending on the thickness and materials of the tank and any protective coatings (Carter, 1984, pp. 17–18).

Medium

Presuming that we have some idea of the level of energy the weapon needs to deliver to the target to produce the particular military effect we have in mind, the next step is to understand how the energy propagates through the medium between the weapon and the target. For targets on or near the earth, the atmosphere normally has the most significant effect. For radio frequency weapons, the ionosphere and the charged-particle environment in space may also be significant.

The idea that propagation conditions vary with weather is as familiar as a cloudy day. The notion that propagation of radiated energy through the atmosphere varies with the wavelength of energy ought to be familiar to anyone who has been sunburned on a cloudy day. Only selected wavelength bands are suitable for space weapons aimed at terrestrial targets. For example, hydrogen fluoride chemical lasers could attack targets only at altitudes above about 14 km. A deuterium fluoride laser or a chemical oxygen iodine laser (COIL) could attack targets down to the surface.

Finally, one aspect of directed-energy propagation that is independent of weather, atmosphere, aerosols, charged particles, or magnetic fields dominates the effectiveness, logistics and basing of space weapons: distance. Even though the energy is focused as tightly as the weapon can project it, its intensity will still decrease in proportion to one over the square of the range from weapon to target.[3] At the great distances to be expected for space weapons, this effect dominates. This inverse square dependence has a profound effect on the combinations of size, number, and altitudes of a weapon constellation that will make sense.

Weapon

If we have a budget for the energy needed at the target for the effect desired, including entries for the uncertainty in the amount needed, coupling into the target, and propagation to the target, we have a basis for sizing a weapon to deliver that energy. For the sake of concreteness, we will use a particular instance of this class of weapon for illustration in this section and the next: a space-based laser. The principles are the same for other kinds of directed-energy weapons. Laser technology represents one of the earliest opportunities to field a lethal space-based directed-energy weapon for terrestrial targets.

The intensity of the energy flux a directed-energy weapon can deliver to a target is a critical sizing parameter. The higher the intensity, the less time it takes to kill a single target. The rate of kills possible in a

---

[3] In short-range cases, in which the focus may result in a spot on the target too small to be confident of causing the desired effect or of hitting a vulnerable part of the target, the weapon may deliberately defocus its beam.

given time is determined by the time for a single kill and the time needed to retarget the weapon to the next target. The kill-rate capacity is critical for sizing weapons, force structures, and counter-measures. A time-honored means of overcoming defenses is to concentrate or mass an attack in space and time to overwhelm the capacity of a defense. For ballistic missiles, concentration can be achieved with salvo launches. For directed-energy weapons, the intensity of directed energy is the fundamental measure of the weapon's capacity to deal with concentration.

The intensity of the energy the weapon can direct to a target depends on a combination of the power the weapon can generate and its ability to concentrate that power at the target. The power the weapon can generate depends on the efficiency and capacity of the means it uses to convert stored or generated energy into the needed form. Energy for a laser may be stored as some combination of chemical fuels and electrical energy. The efficiency of converting the stored form to the directable form will influence the logistics of re-supplying the weapons in orbit (energy or fuel storage and transport). Efficiency varies among different kinds of weapons. Hydrogen fluoride or deuterium fluoride chemical lasers should use of about 2 to 3 kg of fuel per second of operation per megawatt of laser power generated (Velikhov, Sagdeev, and Kokoshin, 1986, p. 29).[4]

The laser's ability to concentrate energy spatially on the target depends primarily on the size of the optics, measured in wavelengths of the energy directed. With allowances for structural elements that may block portions of the optical aperture, the ability to concentrate energy on a small spot at the target improves in proportion to the area of the primary optical surface. Up to the point that the spot size at the target range is too small for the weapon's user to be confident that it will hit something vulnerable, larger optics and shorter wavelengths are better. There are challenges to this. Bigger optics and a smaller spot at the target also mean a need for greater precision in aiming the weapon and a need for a steadier "hand"—that is, mini-

---

[4]*Fuel* includes the diluting gas used to keep the reactant concentrations low enough to prevent detonation. The estimate here represents the middle of the range of efficiencies predicted in the range of references cited. Predictions in the 1980s ranged from 1 to 10 kg/MW.

mizing jitter to keep the smaller spot concentrated on the intended target area.

Within the limits of available technology, bigger optics are logistically preferable to a more powerful laser with smaller optics. In this case, the increase in lethality comes with a one-time transportation cost to put the weapon in space, while a larger laser must have its fuel replenished, a continuing transportation cost. NASA's proposal for a next-generation space telescope is a useful benchmark for space-based laser optics (see Figure 3.1). The spacecraft will use lightweight segmented mirrors, is projected to weigh around 2.5 to 3 metric tons, and will have a diameter of 8 m (GSFC, 1998). When the technology is available for mirrors of that scale, weight, and optical quality in space that are able to withstand the heat of a high-power laser, space-based laser weapons for terrestrial targets will become feasible. When they do, logistic suitability and basing will determine when they become reasonable, as discussed in the next section.

RAND*MR1209-3.1*

**Figure 3.1—Artist's Concept for an 8-m Next-Generation Space Telescope
for Launch Around 2007**

Basing

To illustrate the issues in sizing and basing a space-based laser, we will focus on one stressing mission: boost-phase ballistic missile defense.[5] We will look at one example here. Appendix A explores the variations possible as a function of the missile targets and trajectories and of weapon characteristics, sizing, and orbital basing in more detail. None of the variations has been optimized or designed for an actual threat; they are intended to illustrate broad trends rather than argue for or against specific technologies or designs.

The allure of space-based lasers against such time-urgent targets as ballistic missiles is the possibility of engaging the target sooner, within the atmosphere, thus eliminating the need to characterize the target's probable future trajectory before selecting weapons that can reach it in time. Later discussions will restrict kinetic-energy engagements against missile targets to altitudes above 60 km and will delay weapon release until 30 seconds after the target's launch. The first is needed to keep the kinetic energy interceptor out of the atmosphere. The second is required for predicting the target's trajectory and selecting a suitable weapon. In the laser case, the engagement can occur at an altitude as low as the directed energy can efficiently penetrate. The engagement can begin much sooner after launch because we do not need as much trajectory and signature information to begin an engagement.

Example: Laser for Missile Targets

To illustrate space-based lasers for boost-phase missile defense, we will start with a target damage threshold of 10,000 J/cm^2 and require a hydrogen fluoride laser to deliver that level of energy in a damage

---

[5]The Reagan-era debate over the use of strategic missile defense as an alternative to or an element of nuclear deterrence produced an extensive literature on ballistic missile defense. The discussion here will not revisit all of that material but will focus on some of the issues for the use of space weapons against ballistic missile targets in general. For a balanced, if somewhat dated, tutorial on the general topic of ballistic missile defense in the context of massive nuclear arsenals, see OTA (1985).

spot with a radius no smaller than 10 cm.[6] We will assume the ability to retarget the laser to a new target within 0.5 sec.

Given these parameters, a single laser should, in the 49 seconds from the time the medium-range missile targets reach the laser's 15-km minimum altitude until they burn out, kill about three medium-range ballistic missiles out of a salvo launch from a range of about 1,700 km and a base altitude of 550 km with an aspect angle from its line of sight to the target around 30 degrees off of broadside. So, any salvo of four or more missiles would saturate this laser's defense. The remaining missiles would be able to deploy their warheads. In the process of killing three missiles, the laser might consume about 500 to 750 kg of laser fuel. All the qualifications on this sample statement of capability are a reminder that the actual performance of a constellation of space-based lasers is a dynamic combination of factors that fluctuate over time with contributions from the entire constellation.

Because any one space-based laser may not be in view of the area from which its target missiles are launched at a particular time, we must supply a constellation of lasers to ensure that one or more of them will be in view of potential launch areas in time to engage the targets while they are vulnerable. For this example, the constellation includes 24 space-based lasers at an altitude of 1,248 km. The number of satellites is representative of a relatively small constellation. For missile defense from low earth orbit, laser constellations will number in dozens. Figure 3.2 shows the number of missiles that this example constellation of lasers could kill at any time during the day out of a salvo launch of medium-range ballistic missiles from Korea against Guam.[7] The absolute value of the number killed is less important here than the overall shape over time. If the one to six missiles killed seem disappointing, bear in mind that the number killed could vary by a factor of ten or more with different assumptions about target hardness.

---

[6]The hydrogen fluoride laser is the space-based laser technology that has received the most funding and development.

[7]Appendix B explains the shape of this figure in more detail.

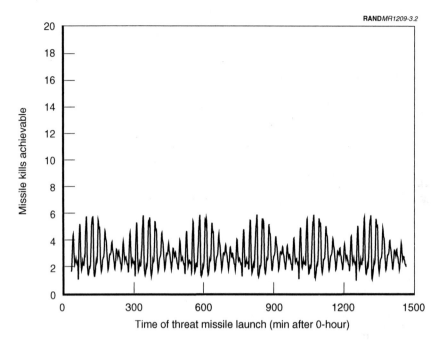

Figure 3.2—Example Space-Based Laser Kill Capacity

Figure 3.2 points out an important aspect of laser performance: The shape of this curve (and thus the timing of its capacity to kill missile targets) is predictable and readily available to any opponent sophisticated enough to have ballistic missiles. The opponent will certainly time missile launches to coincide with the lowest points. Although the opponent may not be confident of how hard his missiles are against the power of the lasers (and so of the minimum salvo size needed to have some penetrate), he will be certain of the timing of his best opportunities—which will be regular and frequent. This is not something the owner of the space-based lasers can prevent.

Because of their size, the lasers would be extremely difficult to hide or to maneuver enough to be unpredictable. While it would be fairly easy to field a capability to track the lasers, Internet access would probably make owning a space tracking system unnecessary because amateur astronomers are likely to publish the orbital data on line.[8]

Claims about laser constellation lethality should be checked carefully for their assumptions about the timing of launch. A maximum kill rate assumes that the opponent is willfully self-destructive. An average kill rate assumes that the opponent is blissfully oblivious. Only a claim of minimum performance is reasonable for this class of time-urgent targets. Any apparent excess of maximum over minimum kill rate capacity is surplus or wasted (at least for this target). Appendix A discusses weapon and constellation design approaches that could reduce the sources of variation in kill rate capacity in more detail.

For less-urgent targets or alternative missions in which the laser's owner can choose the time and geometry of engagement, this surplus target capacity could be put to use without compromising the constellation's capability against the ballistic missile targets. For example, a laser whose wavelength is chosen to penetrate low enough into the atmosphere could be used against airplanes or cruise missiles in flight or even against terrestrial targets, such as aboveground fuel tanks, missiles still on their launchers or transporters, fuel trucks, and other relatively thin-skinned or flammable targets. To the degree that such targets are vulnerable to the kind of surface-heating damage that a laser can inflict, they should require amounts of laser fuel to engage that are similar to those required for a missile target,[9] although the laser could presumably pick the times of engagement to take advantage of the shortest ranges to target. Of course, any use of the excess kill-rate capacity would still have to fit within the logistic limits of energy storage (electrical or chemical) and replenishment.

The lethality of a constellation of such weapons fluctuates dynamically and predictably. Yet the situation is essentially static because, like an interlocking network of fortifications on the ground, the pre-

---

[8]SeeSat-L is an example. The site advertises itself as "the Internet mailing list for visual satellite observers. . . . SeeSat-L has become an almost invaluable tool for the satellite observer," providing up-to-date orbital elements for U.S. spy satellites, MIR, the Space Shuttle, and others (Clifford and DePontieu, 1994).

[9]Or possibly less for nonlethal and indirect effects such as illumination or stimulating fluorescence in aircraft canopy materials to degrade the pilot's view out of the cockpit.

dictability cannot be altered once the satellites are in orbit. Like any static defense, a constellation can be saturated by attacks that are sufficiently concentrated in space and time. And determined opponents will evolve the weapons and tactics to do so.

A space-based laser constellation should therefore be augmented by weapons and tactics that blunt the opponent's opportunity to saturate or that bring additional resources to bear in response to such an attempt. It will not be reasonable to concentrate directed-energy weapons in orbit. It may be reasonable to augment them with terrestrial and atmospheric platforms, if such platforms can be in place in time. It will certainly help to add layers, such as the kinetic-energy interceptors discussed in the next section and conventional surface-based interceptors, to concentrate on the leakage through the static defense. Taking advantage of the longer time it takes missiles to be assembled and prepared for a salvo would allow taking the fight to the opponent to reduce his ability to mount a concentrated attack—if weapon design (wavelength selection) and weather permit. Missiles prepositioned in hardened silos or bunkers would be attacked using kinetic-energy rods or conventional weapons, as we will discuss in later sections of this chapter.

Some degree of reserve capacity might be useful for a directed-energy weapon constellation—if the excess can be applied against useful targets. For example, the reserve capacity could be available for taking the fight to the opponent, against the targets and at the times one chooses. Focusing on only the most urgent mission—for example, by selecting a wavelength that does not propagate to potential targets of interest or by overoptimizing weapon and orbit selections—could easily cause one to miss the opportunity to concentrate such a reserve.

For some problems, the static limitations of such a constellation may be desirable, possibly essential. There is, however, such a thing as too much defense. In the current context, the issue is national missile defense against a limited threat—accidental or rogue nation launch—since mutual deterrence of nuclear war is already in place among peers. To avoid destabilizing deterrence among peers, the defense must not be too capable (Wilkening, 2000). Whereas deployable terrestrial defenses may be ambiguous in their application to theater defenses and national defense, a space-based directed-energy defense would be observably limited.

MASS-TO-TARGET WEAPONS

The important military issues in delivering mass to a target are the suitability of the destructive effect to the reason for engaging the target (including certainty and timeliness of the effect and avoiding unintended consequences) and the logistics of delivering the effect on target (both transportation delay and expense). When the delivery is from space to a target on earth, the suitability and logistics are dominated by the Keplerian dynamics of motion outside the atmosphere in the earth's gravity well and the dynamics of reentry through the atmosphere from orbital speeds, both of which are generally unfamiliar. The discussion that follows will try to make the influence of these dynamics on weapon effects and employment more familiar; Appendix B provides more detail. Before discussing the challenging problem of atmospheric reentry, we will first cover the use of weapons against targets leaving the atmosphere, which is a logical progression from the previous section's discussion of boost-phase ballistic missile defense. This kind of weapon might provide a defensive layer to engage targets that leak through the laser's boost-phase defense.

General Characteristics

We will review three different kinds of space-based weapons that deliver mass to a target for destructive effect. One is confined to targets above or leaving the atmosphere. The two others have to penetrate the atmosphere to reach targets. For all three, there is a transportation cost for basing in orbit rather than on the ground. Depending on the base orbit, the additional transportation effort is equivalent to the effort needed to deliver a short- to medium-range ballistic missile.

Moreover, if the user cannot choose when to use the weapon, another potentially big penalty comes into play: If the timing is urgent, the absentee ratio may be large. Depending on the nature of the weapon and the urgency of delivering it to target, absentee ratios for orbital basing can range from a handful (comparable to theater-range terrestrial platforms) to dozens.

Space basing is more responsive than the alternatives. Independent of the economics, operational necessity, such as the need to differentiate nuclear weapons from others, may drive a preference for space basing over more economical long-range ballistic missiles.

These weapons do not require particularly exotic materials or technology. Anyone who has developed ICBMs or spacecraft and, for the missile interceptors, air or missile defenses has the ability to develop and produce mass-to-target weapons. For that matter, their development for space basing could reasonably be concealed within conventional programs. Only large-scale deployment in space might be obvious.

Kinetic-Energy Weapons Above the Atmosphere

Here, the weapon and basing issues are very different from those for the terrestrial targets described later in this chapter. Because the most interesting and challenging use of these weapons is for missile defense (much as discussed above under space-based lasers), the issues are similar. Against the urgent targets of ballistic missiles leaving the atmosphere, basing must be at low altitude, and absentee ratios begin at the level of several dozens. Against that target class, this kind of weapon is best employed in concert with others (like the space-based lasers of the previous section) that reduce the urgency and extend the utility of this weapon's contribution. Because the entire engagement occurs outside the atmosphere, these weapons can be very small because they kill by hitting their targets at a very high velocity. Small size helps to reduce the cost of the additional propulsion needed for each weapon to leave its orbital base.

Targets. For targets that can be usefully intercepted at altitudes above about 60 km, the atmosphere is not important for weapon choice. Instead, what drives the logistics here is the time available to complete the intercept, which begins with commitment of the kinetic-energy weapon to a target (after launch detection and characterization) and ends when intercept is no longer possible or useful. If the target missile has a single warhead, the end could be as late as reentry into the atmosphere—if an intercept that late would reliably destroy the target's potential to do harm.

But interception might not reliably eliminate all the destructive potential of a target carrying chemical or biological agents, particularly if the payload is intentionally fractionated. Some hazardous debris might survive reentry. Most would be dispersed over a very broad area by winds in the atmosphere, its harmful effects made more diffuse, perhaps acceptably so, depending on the nature of the agent and the environmental effects of chemistry, temperature, and solar radiation on the agent as it disperses and falls. If a "late" intercept would not decrease the target weapon's effects to an acceptable level,[10] it would be important to intercept the target soon enough for the debris to fall as far from its intended impact point (or as close to its launch point) as possible. As a deterrent, the possibility of poisoning one's own homeland should give a rational actor more reason not to employ such weapons.

If the missile carries a fractionating payload, it should be intercepted while it is still boosting, before it has the opportunity to deploy its warheads or decoys and increase the number of aim points. This would, in addition, allow the interceptor to home in on the bright signature of the booster's exhaust, and cause any debris from the intercept to fall closer to the launch point. Depending on the range and the design of the missile, the duration of boost can vary substantially from about 1 to 5 minutes (Carter et al., 1984, p. 52; OTA, 1985, pp. 156, 173). The shorter times occur for shorter range missiles or for hypothetical, but possible, "fast-burn, long-range" missiles. Some of that boost time, perhaps 30 seconds, would be needed to detect the launch, characterize the trajectory (and possibly the vehicle by its propulsion characteristics), and select weapons capable of reaching it in time.

Weapon. Since the destructive kinetic energy results from the combination of the target ballistic missile's high velocity (reaching several kilometers per second) with the weapon's velocity, we can

---

[10]*Late,* in this case, does not mean over the target area but late enough in the boost phase, while still over the launch area, that the ballistic path of the debris continuing outside of the atmosphere after the intercept would still reach the vicinity of the intended target area.

minimize the mass of the interceptor. The minimum mass may be little more than the weight of the sensor and propulsion needed to complete intercept once accelerated to the speed necessary to reach the target in time from its initial orbital location. From the interceptor's point of view, an intercept on the downward part of the missile's trajectory may be preferable, since the geometry could allow the interceptor to view the target against the cold, dark background of space. Since the contrast would be better than against an earth background, sensing and homing on the target would be easier.

Basing. Except for "fast-burn" missiles, the target missile burns out at an altitude somewhere between 200 and 400 km, where atmospheric drag on a satellite either would require it to have substantial additional propulsion or would quickly shorten its life. So, to intercept the target before burnout, the interceptor will need to shoot down from its base altitude, which will need to be as low as possible.

To see how critical the allowable time for the intercept is, consider the following: A base altitude of 500 km and an available time of 330 sec to strike a missile target at an altitude of 200 km, and interceptor propulsion magnitude similar to that of a medium-range ballistic missile would require an absentee factor of about 60 for global coverage. But with a propulsion magnitude similar to that of an ICBM, the absentee ratio could be about 30. As the time the interceptor has to reach its target at a given altitude decreases, the effort needed to do so increases greatly and rapidly begins to exceed what rocket propulsion can reasonably supply. At some point, accelerating the interceptors would require more exotic propulsion technology, such as electromagnetic guns.

If this weapon class were the only contributor to boost-phase missile defense, opposing technology developments for faster-burn missiles could quickly make them outmoded. If, on the other hand, the urgency of intercept is limited, perhaps by sharing some of the boost-phase problem with other classes, such as lasers, and if the engagement window is opened to include the full extent of the ballistic missile's trajectory outside the atmosphere, this kinetic-energy weapon could contribute effectively to a layered missile defense. However, like all space-based defenses, it would be static and thus subject to saturation by a determined opponent, even with the extended opportunity to engage targets throughout their flight outside the atmosphere.

Kinetic-Energy Weapons Against Terrestrial Targets

These weapons also use only their own mass and very high velocity to create a destructive effect. However, unlike kinetic-energy weapons operating outside the atmosphere, those for use against surface targets must be large enough to survive reentry through the atmosphere with the high velocity they need for their destructive effect. A reasonable starting point for estimating their size and costs would be the upper stage of a multiple-warhead, independently targetable reentry vehicle ballistic missile—including the reentry vehicles but minus the warheads. Adjustments would have to be made for the power and thermal effects of extended orbital life, maneuver magnitude, commanding, different guidance, and production volume.

Because of their extremely high velocity, these weapons are very difficult to defend against during their brief transit through the atmosphere and might therefore be particularly interesting against heavily defended targets. These weapons may be of only limited interest to the United States, which has other means of global power projection. However, they may be a very good fit for another country, such as one seeking global power projection without duplicating the U.S. terrestrial investment or one seeking to deny access to U.S. power projection forces. For example, instead of playing catch-up against highly evolved air and submarine defenses, a country might prefer these space weapons to bypass the defense entirely.

Targets. Because they must be long and slender to retain their high kinetic energy through the atmosphere and yet have reasonable weights, these weapons would be useful only for targets susceptible to the kind of damage a vertically penetrating weapon can inflict. Suitable targets would include tall buildings, missile silos, ships,[11] and hardened aircraft shelters but not runways; deeply buried

---

[11]If the ships cannot move too far unpredictably in the few seconds it takes for weapon reentry.

bunkers; bridges[12]; and long, low buildings.[13] For most susceptible targets, defense against this kind of weapon would be very difficult inside the atmosphere. Burying is the best defense for fixed surface targets, but other armor is unlikely to be practical. Alternatively, an opponent with an appropriate surveillance capability could find these weapons in space and attack them before they can release penetrators.

Medium. Rodlike reentry vehicles face two significant problems in transiting the atmosphere that impose peculiar basing constraints: Making sure that they can survive the intense heat of very rapid reentry and that they *fall*, not *fly*.

To address the first problem, the vehicles will generally require active cooling, extruding material through pores in their nosetips for evaporation. Relying on ablative cooling—the melting away of an outer layer—would run into the second problem.

At the high velocities of reentry, any aerodynamic behavior will cause large, unpredictable misses, even if the rod survives unexpected changes in heat and structural loading from flying. Ablation would erode the nose unevenly and unpredictably. The rods must remain symmetrical to avoid any tendency to fly. They also need to be delivered with a zero angle of attack to minimize any tendency to fly. This constrains their trajectory outside the atmosphere, requiring them to enter it close to vertically.

Weapons. Among the kinds of space weapons that rely on delivering mass to the target, the kinetic-energy weapon is one with a counterpart in nature: the meteoroid.[14] This natural counterpart, although too destructive to be useful, provides a starting point for scaling to the more modest effects desired for man-made weapons. One significant difference between meteoroids and nuclear weapons is that the meteoroid leaves no radioactive debris. Among the other differences significant for understanding kinetic-energy weapons are the sizes of meteoroids and their velocities.

---

[12]Unless enough weapons are used to be confident of hitting a vulnerable point.

[13]Unless the buildings are filled with flammables.

[14]Note that, although there are technical distinctions between the terms meteor, meteorite, and meteoroid, we prefer meteoroid for ease of discussion.

Meteoroids encounter the earth's atmosphere at 11 to 70 km per second (Bjork, 1961). Those that survive the trip through the earth's atmosphere may be as small as a gram, but the result is more like dust settling than a weapon impacting. In contrast, the crater-makers start at around 300 metric tons yet leave only small fragments behind after they hit (Dodd, 1986). The largest of the three craters at Wabar, Saudi Arabia, was caused by a fragment in the range of 3,000 metric tons (Wynn and Shoemaker, 1998), the smallest by one about 4 metric tons.[15] The Barringer meteor crater in Arizona is a little over 1 km wide and was caused by an iron meteor with a diameter of about 15 to 20 m and a mass of about 18,000 to 62,000 metric tons (Bjork, 1961). At the extreme end of the range (in notoriety if not size) is the 10- to 20-km–wide stony meteorite that left a 170-km-diameter crater in the Yucatan peninsula (Hamilton and Hamilton, 1995). This impact is the one associated with the Alvarez hypothesis on the extinction of the dinosaurs.

Fortunately, as Appendix C explains, natural meteoroids cannot reasonably be considered as weapons, despite their potential for enormous destruction. A reasonably sized kinetic-energy weapon to place in space would be larger than dust but would preferably weigh less than tons and would have less-drastic effects than mass extinction. In between the dust and the crater-makers are objects that slow down enough through the atmosphere to survive impact.

Low-drag reentry vehicle technology for ICBMs provides a useful middle ground. The approach here is to make a small, solid, long, and narrow reentry vehicle out of a high-density material.[16] For example, one such weapon might be a 1-m-long tungsten rod weighing about 100 kg. The rod would actually be a slender, sphere-capped cone with a nose radius of about 1 cm and a cone half-angle of about a couple of degrees. It should be able to penetrate about 1.5 m of steel, almost 3 m of clay or stone, and only 1 m of uranium. Reactive armor should not be effective against it, because the rod is solid behind the leading edge eroding its way into the target material. What penetrates through that depth (or less) of target will be a very hot mixture of target and penetrator material and any remaining pene-

---

[15]The craters have diameters of 116, 60, and 11 m.

[16]Appendix B provides the details of sizing, materials, and basing.

trator length, still moving at high velocity. As with a shaped-charge explosive, the damage is done almost entirely in the direction of the impact, except for damage from fires or explosions secondary to the impact.[17] The shock wave of the impact will also cause some spalling of brittle target materials, such as concrete, as it propagates forward. This would turn an otherwise nearly cylindrical penetration into a narrow (of about 30 degree) cone opening up from the point of impact.

Basing. Space-based kinetic-energy weapons incur a number of other constraints that become important for basing. In addition to a steep reentry angle, these weapons need to be delivered to have enough velocity on entering the atmosphere to have a lethal terminal velocity. But within these constraints, there are orbital options. The task in selecting the orbit is to minimize the number of platforms and the logistic effort required to put them in orbit and deorbit them yet achieve the desired degree of responsiveness and reach. For global or hemispheric reach, the responsiveness can reasonably be a few hours for the logistic effort needed to deliver a single weapon, which is similar to that for a large ICBM.

The fuel required to emplace and deorbit the weapons might be about 50 times the mass of the weapons delivered. This compares with a reported fuel-consumption ratio of 40 tons per ton of air-delivered ordnance in the Gulf War (Scales, 1999, pp. xvi, 88). The absentee ratio needed for global access would be about 6, and for hemispheric coverage, about half that. These are similar to absentee ratios for terrestrial platforms.

Note that the responsiveness limits still allow much more timely target updates. Targeting adjustments are possible throughout the flight outside the atmosphere, and small changes are possible up to a few tens of seconds before impact. This could make large, slowly moving targets, such as ships, vulnerable if their maneuvers could be observed, either by the weapon dispensing platform or, more likely, by other satellites.

---

[17]While solid tungsten is not pyrophoric at room temperature, hot tungsten vapor, liquid droplets, and small solid particles will combust. The portion of a penetrator that reaches atmosphere inside the target (say, in a bunker or the interior of a ship) in a combustible form will act like an explosive charge.

In selecting orbital basing for weapons to be deorbited to strike terrestrial targets, the survivability of the weapons and difficulty of defending against them will depend on how difficult the chosen base makes surveillance. The difficulty of detecting the initiation of an attack depends on the volume of space to be watched, the duration of the observable event, and the detectability of the event's signature. Detectability will depend on the intensity of the signal, its contrast against the background, and the distance its energy must propagate.

For example, looking down at a continental landmass to detect long-range ballistic missile launches requires only one or two high-altitude satellites with moderately sized sensors that scan the landmass a few times a minute. The sensors should see the hot exhaust of missiles that burn for several minutes against the background of the earth and track them well enough to characterize the event with some confidence. From three to six such satellites could watch the entire globe.[18]

On the other hand, detecting a rocket firing that deorbits a space-based weapon might require about two dozen low-altitude satellites with much wider fields of view and more-capable sensors that stare at the volume of space around and above them or scan it rapidly enough to be confident of seeing a deorbit burn that lasts a fraction of that of a long-range ballistic missile.[19] Depending on the altitude of the space weapon's orbital base, the deorbit burn might last about one-fifth that of an ICBM launch.

Basing at higher altitudes increases the volume of space to be watched, increases the distance from terrestrial sensors, and decreases the magnitude of the maneuver needed to deorbit. On the negative side, such bases increase the total effort required to em-

---

[18]The U.S. Defense Support Program is one such constellation, a missile warning system described on line at http://www.losangeles.af.mil/SMC/MT/DSP/HISTORY/Dsppg01c.htm.

[19]Such a constellation would be similar to the Space-Based Infrared System-Low (SBIRS-Low) component of the current program to replace U.S. missile warning satellites. The difference is that SBIRS-Low is intended to have a surveillance sensor looking down for ballistic missile launches and a track sensor able to follow detected launches through trajectory after burnout. A system to detect space-based deorbit rocket firings would need surveillance sensors oriented toward space. A description of the SBIRS-Low concept is available on line at http://www.losangeles.af.mil/SMC/MT/BROCHURE/brochure.htm.

place and deorbit a weapon and increase the delay between a decision to strike and the impact on a target.

Conventional Weapons Against Terrestrial Targets

Adding the option to use conventional munitions against terrestrial targets changes the issues considerably. The targets for this class of weapon depend on the capabilities of the conventional munitions delivered to the proximity of their targets from their bases in space.[20]

Conventional weapons delivered from space against terrestrial targets inherit the lethality and utility of their fundamental design. But because delivering them to targets from space is more expensive logistically, only those that are precise and accurate and, therefore, of small mass are likely to be interesting for orbital basing. For this group, the responsiveness of orbital basing can reasonably be about 20 to 30 min, with an absentee ratio of about 6 for global access. The costs of basing such weapons in space for this purpose are sensitive to the packaging and aerodynamic performance on reentry. In this regard, early film-return or astronaut capsules would be a useful starting point for less-expensive, lower-performance weapon packaging, and advanced maneuverable reentry vehicles for more-expensive, higher-performance packaging.

Targets. Our discussion of kinetic-energy weapons against terrestrial targets focused on targets fixed on the ground or moving slowly enough that they would not escape the footprint of a cluster of weapons aimed at them in the few seconds between the last opportunity to adjust the weapons' trajectory outside the atmosphere and impact. Although reentry vehicles can maneuver extensively through the atmosphere at the expense of significant complexity and some loss of kinetic energy, their maneuver is better suited to complicating the task of defenses or to correcting guidance errors against fixed targets than to following dynamic targets. Aside from the very high speed and short duration of reentry, which make intercept difficult, a

---

[20]*Conventional munitions* could include rather exotic munitions, including such things as radio-frequency or high-power-microwave munitions, such as those described in "Just a Normal Town" (2000). The key attribute here is that the weapons require physical delivery to the proximity of the target without retaining the high velocity associated with hypervelocity kill mechanisms.

sheath of hot, ionized atmosphere around the reentry vehicle effectively isolates it from sensing or communication for critical periods of reentry.[21] However, if a reentry vehicle decreases its velocity to deploy a conventional submunition, the ability to engage maneuvering targets would depend on the capability of the submunition to find and reach its target. For example, a smart anti-tank submunition dispensed from a reentry vehicle should be as effective as it would be if it had been dispensed from a cruise missile or aircraft.

In addition to attacking targets that maneuver more rapidly, conventional ordnance delivered from space could attack targets not accessible to kinetic-energy weapons. This includes surface targets that require the destructive force to be directed outward, as opposed to downward, from the point of impact, as well as targets that are more deeply buried. Slower-speed penetrators do not erode in the same way as the hypervelocity rods discussed in the last section. However, they do require explosives and fusing that can survive the impact and determine the correct depth of penetration for detonation.

Because these weapons have a longer, slower reentry and have conventional weapon characteristics after being deployed from reentry vehicles, they are more susceptible to terminal defenses than the kinetic-energy weapons would be. For basing orbits with attractive combinations of logistic effort and responsiveness, defense against them outside the atmosphere would have less time to work with after deorbit starts but easier reach from the earth beforehand.

Medium. For conventional weapons delivered from space, the atmosphere is less of a challenge and something of an opportunity. Unlike a kinetic-energy weapon, a conventional-weapon reentry vehicle would deliberately prolong its transit through the atmosphere, starting at shallower reentry angles and maneuvering (or modulating its shape) to increase drag at higher altitudes to reduce the intense heat load on the vehicle at denser, lower altitudes. The atmospheric lift and drag that were a problem for kinetic-energy weapons are the means of achieving an expanded footprint, a cooler vehicle, and the transition to conditions suitable for dispensing the conventional weapons in the vicinity of their targets. If footprint flexibility were

---

[21]The exception would be inertial sensing, which does not require electromagnetic energy propagation through the plasma sheath.

not worth the added complexity of maneuver, using a simpler, less expensive, blunt design for the reentry vehicle could yield the same cooler reentry and transition to slower, even subsonic, conditions for dispensing munitions.

Weapon. Again in contrast with kinetic-energy weapons, lethality no longer depends on retaining high velocity and a steep angle of reentry but rather on the accuracy of targeting and maneuver after reentry. An example of a conventional weapon that might be particularly suitable is the Low Cost Autonomous Attack System (LOCAAS), a miniature airplane that has a laser radar to sense and identify targets, a range under powered flight of about 100 mi after deployment, and a "self-forging" warhead capable of adapting to different targets and ranges by assuming long-rod penetrator, aerodynamic penetrator, or multiple fragment shapes (Barela, 1996).

For conventional weapons that have their own means of terminal maneuver and guidance to target once released from the reentry vehicle, a simple, blunt design would be logistically more efficient than a winged or lifting-body reentry vehicle. A shape capable of carrying a large number of smart munitions might resemble a larger version of the original Discoverer/Corona film return capsules. The first of these capsules successfully recovered is shown in Figure 3.3. The technology for this kind of reentry vehicle is old and widely available. The technology for the submunitions that it would deliver is newer.

Basing. For space basing of these weapons, timely response and long reach are still in conflict with each other, but the conflict has a happier resolution than it did with kinetic-energy weapons. Because steep reentry angles and high reentry velocities are not constraints (or even desirable) for conventional weapons, the base orbits can be substantially lower to increase responsiveness without reducing footprint. For example, if the goal is continuous, global access to targets, an absentee ratio of about 5 at a 500 km altitude and with a responsiveness of about a half hour from decision to destruction should be possible. This would be possible for roughly the same level of total effort to deliver a weapon as that for kinetic-energy weapons.

National Air and Space Museum, Smithsonian Institution (SI A-47680-A).

Figure 3.3—President Eisenhower Viewing Discoverer 13 Capsule

This combination of responsiveness and reach is similar to that possible with long-range ballistic missiles, which would require equivalent or less effort to deliver to target. Long-range ballistic missiles would also have no logistic penalty for absentee ratio. The principal argument against using them to deliver conventional weapons is concern that they might be confused with nuclear weapons.

One might think that space launch vehicles could be confused with ballistic missiles during launch. However, basing location, number launched at one time, and signature (infrared intensity over time) indicate the vehicle type at launch. As the launch proceeds, when tracking no longer provides a predicted impact point on the earth, i.e., when the trajectory achieves orbit, there is no doubt that the launch is a spacecraft rather than a ballistic missile.

Aircraft, cruise missiles, and shorter-range ballistic missiles that have a historical association with nuclear weapons have later been used for conventional warheads without that confusion. Some—such as the B-52, B-1, and B-2 bombers, the air-launched cruise missile, and the Tomahawk cruise missile—have been converted from nuclear warheads to conventional warheads while retaining nuclear capability. If the kind of responsiveness and reach possible with long-range ballistic missiles is desirable, it should be possible to avoid the confusion with nuclear weapons through some combination of vehicle characteristics, operational practice, basing, and arms control. Achieving distinguishable vehicle characteristics might be a natural consequence of developing a vehicle similar to a ballistic missile but with better economy, possibly through reuse or derivation from a space-launch vehicle.

Chapter Four

EMPLOYMENT

It may seem premature to discuss employment issues for weapons that the United States has not even decided to acquire, but such issues are a necessary part of defining and understanding proposed new capabilities, particularly those that exploit technologies that are not widely understood. This chapter will argue that an understanding of space weapons must relate their technical characteristics to their possible uses and command structure. This is important for several reasons.

First, deciding whether to acquire new capabilities should be grounded in an understanding of how they could be made most useful to the warfighting commanders. The current space-based laser program, for example, uses a technology that cannot engage targets low in the atmosphere because of its specific wavelength. A discussion that focuses on this particular program would not include a number of possible uses of space-based lasers in warfare. Similarly, even if the space-based laser discussion included wavelengths that penetrated further into the atmosphere, a system acquired for a command structure tailored to national missile defense might not be usable for theater missile or air defense.

Second, the consideration of how a weapon could best be employed should be a key factor in deciding *what* to acquire—i.e., the weapon's size, number, and characteristics. For example, should a space-based conventional-weapon dispenser be a highly maneuverable aerodynamic reentry vehicle carrying only two or three "silver bullet" submunitions for extremely high-value targets, or should it be a large, blunt capsule with drag augmentation designed to carry as large a load of tank-killing submunitions as possible? How many kinetic-energy penetrators should be packaged on a dispenser with how large a cross-range footprint for how many of what kinds of targets? How do the apportionment, planning, release, and abort of kinetic and conventional weapons from space fit into cycles for planning and using other forces for engaging those targets? Decisions on the last three issues would constrain the options available to warfighters for the life of the constellations of weapons acquired. How diffuse a spot should a space-based laser be able to illuminate and with what intensity? What wavelength should a laser have to engage what targets? How much reserve capacity should a space-based laser have for other targets? How should it be allocable to what uses? What combination of on-orbit fuel and resupply should a laser constellation have? The answers to these questions all depend on how the weapons are going to be employed.

Third, focusing on the technical characteristics of a proposed weapon program without considering how the weapon would be used runs the risk of having weapons that are ineffective in the field or that cannot be readily apportioned among the commanders who need them. Among the more-notable historical examples of this problem is the original use of the machine gun by the French in the Franco-Prussian War of 1870. The French had developed their Gatling-gun-like *mitrailleuse* in secrecy (O'Connell, 1989). When it was ready, the French treated it like an artillery piece, deploying it in the rear with other artillery, where it could not reach infantry targets effectively but could itself be reached by Prussian artillery. The machine gun was not employed compellingly by Western armies until World War I, and then first by the Germans (Brodie and Brodie, 1973, p.145). There is a real possibility that an existing military acquiring space weapons might, much like the 19th-century French, employ them according to the doctrines and customs for other weapons—which may be the wrong sort of example for space weapons. The purpose of this chapter is to suggest, instead, a thoughtful consideration of the similarities, differences, and constraints peculiar to different kinds of space weapons for different uses, rather than simply basing doctrine on the general attributes of the space environment or adopting a custom from any other realm of experience.

EMPLOYMENT

The previous chapter described the technical possibilities of four distinct categories of space weapons: directed-energy weapons, kinetic-energy weapons outside the atmosphere, kinetic-energy weapons within the atmosphere, and conventional weapons delivered from space. The targets and effects for some of these weapons are narrowly defined, but the full collection spans a broad range of capabilities with a diverse set of constraints. To see that breadth in employment, consider the range of functions or tasks to which they might contribute in concert with other means of achieving the same functions and tasks.

Functions and Tasks

The defining distinction between the technical and tactical levels of conflict is the addition of enemy action in the context of the battlefield to the isolated, theoretical interaction of weapon and target. In the theoretical isolation of the technical level, it seems possible simply to match weapons to targets—for example, "use space-based lasers to destroy theater ballistic missiles in the boost phase." But in the real world, it is also necessary to consider the opponent and any of his independent actions. It is thus also necessary to consider aggregations of weapons and tasks into functions.[1] For example, if the opponent adapts to the above ballistic missile defense task by attempting to saturate laser missile defenses with salvo launches and competing aim points,[2] the tactical-level response should include all the elements of the counter-air function. Otherwise, the opponent's action may render the technical-level contribution of the laser irrelevant.

---

[1]The usage here follows the recent U.S. joint doctrine definitions of the terms *roles*, *missions*, and *functions*. A *mission* is a task assigned by the National Command Authorities to a combatant command. A *function* is a specific responsibility assigned to a service (or Special Operations Command) to organize, train, and equip forces for the combatant commands. The *roles* of the services are the broad, enduring purposes for which the services are established in law (JCS, 1997). Earlier versions of doctrine used the term *mission* to describe the counter-air, -sea, -land, etc., activities now called functions.

[2]Perhaps not with decoy ballistic missile launches (which would be difficult to create inexpensively) but perhaps with aircraft, cruise missiles, and decoy cruise missiles (which could be less expensive) added to the ballistic missile salvo.

Conversely, the space weapon's contribution to the counter-air function could include the addition of tasks from other space weapons and other targets, such as the following:

- Destroy aircraft and cruise missiles in flight with space-based lasers.

- Destroy ballistic missiles leaking through laser defenses with kinetic-energy weapons outside the atmosphere.

- Destroy ballistic missiles on transporters and missile propellant trucks en route to salvo launch points with space-based lasers or space-based smart munitions.

- Destroy ballistic and cruise missiles and aircraft in protective structures with space-based kinetic-energy penetrators.

The value of embedding the tasks in this way is that it forces consideration of the opponent's responses in the broader context of alternative or contributing means (air, land, or naval), when they are available.

Exploring other functions yields opportunities for space weapons to contribute to several. Table 4.1 lists some theoretical contributions. A quick inspection reveals that few of these functions could be supported solely by space weapons.[3] For example, counter-sea requires weapons suitable for undersea targets. Although it seems possible to use reentry vehicles to deliver antisubmarine torpedoes from space, they would need targeting information from acoustic sensors on local air, surface, or subsurface platforms that could just as well carry torpedoes themselves.[4]

---

[3]The counter-space contributions from space could be comprehensive but would benefit from contributions by terrestrial forces—such as ground-based satellite uplink jammers, terrestrial weapons in reach of launch and control facilities, direct-ascent antisatellite weapons—when those are more economical. While not strictly terrestrial conflict, the counter-space function belongs in the list of theater functions any time space weapons or capabilities contribute to the theater conflict.

[4]If the logistics of maintaining the mass of weapons more centrally were competitive (in the case of air platforms, because of the expense of maintaining mass aloft or, in the case of surface and subsurface platforms because of the speed of deployment), there might be a combination of local sensors and space-based weapons in the abstract, but the possibility seems unlikely.

Table 4.1

Space Weapon Contributions to Military Functions

For Countering	Directed Energy[a]	Exoatmospheric Kinetic Energy	Endoatmospheric Kinetic Energy	Conventional Ordnance From Space
Air	Destroy ballistic missiles pre-launch and boost phase, aircraft and cruise missiles in flight. Jam air defense sensors and communications	Destroy ballistic missiles post–boost phase	Destroy missiles and aircraft in hardened shelters	Destroy missiles and support vehicles prelaunch
Sea	Destroy aircraft and missile threats to naval forces in flight		Destroy or disable surface ships in port and at sea and supporting shore infrastructure susceptible to vertical penetration	Destroy or disable surface ships in port and at sea and supporting shore infrastructure
Land	Interdict thin-skinned vehicles susceptible to ignition[b]		Destroy fixed targets susceptible to vertical penetration[c]	Interdict mechanized forces in transit and logistics stores and convoys
Information	Jam (or burn out susceptible components) of sensors and communications links		Destroy command bunkers (if not deeply buried)	Destroy communications nodes
Space	Destroy launch vehicles, satellites, and interceptors. Deny navigation signals to satellites. Jam satellite up- down- and/or cross-links. Blind or block satellite sensors	Destroy launch vehicles, satellites, and interceptors attacking satellites	Destroy launch and control facilities	Destroy launch and control facilities

[a]For example, laser, radio frequency.

[b]For example, fuel transport.

[c]e.g., munitions storage, POL storage, bunkers, office buildings, etc.

The counter-land contributions could be as complete as the kinds and numbers of munitions deployed in space would allow. However, the logistic expense of delivering them from space would likely restrict their utility to relatively higher-value targets, e.g., armored vehicle concentrations, not individual, dismounted infantry. Similarly, the cost of using a space-based laser to destroy a fuel tanker truck might be too expensive, given that the laser reactant used would have to be replenished by launching the equivalent of a small satellite—unless the target carried a high value in the harm it could do. For example, the fuel in one tanker of a convoy resupplying a tank column might not be worth the equivalent of a several-million-dollar space launch. But if the tanker were carrying rocket propellant and was in the process of fueling a ballistic missile ready to launch weapons of mass destruction, using a laser to destroy it might be well worth the cost of replenishing the laser.

Alternatively, a space weapon might be the weapon of choice for an otherwise lower-value target if the space weapon were the only choice available in time, particularly for a time-critical political effect. For example, a locomotive might not be worth a space-delivered smart munition. However, it might be well worth the use of a space-delivered smart munition to target a locomotive pulling a train full of people forced from their homes for transport to the border or to a concentration camp at the beginning of an ethnic-cleansing campaign—particularly if aircraft and helicopters cannot reach the train because air defenses have not been suppressed, basing and overflight rights have not been granted, or coalition consensus on the action has not been reached.

Defensive counter-air contributions could be quite extensive if weather conditions permit directed-energy weapons to propagate to atmospheric targets or if air targets are susceptible to the energy that can be delivered at wavelengths able to propagate through the weather. For some ballistic missile threats (e.g., fast-burning, early fractionating missiles launched out of reach of airborne lasers), an attack from space might be the only effective means. Space-based weapons could contribute to the offensive counter-air function as extensively as to the counter-land function, depending on the kinds and numbers of munitions deployed in space.

Component and Sequence

The operational level of conflict encompasses not only the effects of the opponent's actions but the opportunity (sometimes the necessity) to sequence and coordinate the actions of multiple forces from diverse components—air, land, sea, and space—of the joint forces available. At the theater level, the actions of the forces are set in a specific geographical context. The sequence of actions is designed to meet objectives tied more directly to the broad political aims of the conflict. Both the sequence and the combination with diverse land, sea, and air operations are of interest for understanding the employment of space forces.

One could imagine special, limited cases in which the employment of space forces could occur in isolation from other forces.[5] However, such limited use in isolation would likely be incidental to having the space weapons for more general use when sequence and combination of employment with other forces matter.

Use of space weapons in an area might also be a brief prelude to joint operations. The fact that extended air campaigns, such as the 1999 war in Yugoslavia over Kosovo, have occurred with the success of the campaign ruling out a ground component, suggests the possibility of some kind of extended space weapon campaign. However, that possibility presupposes that the relative logistic expense trade-offs have made space weapons competitive with air forces or that political and basing constraints have made use of space weapons necessary. The possibility seems remote at this time.

The most attractive attribute of space forces is their availability on short notice without the need to ask permission for access or the need for a substantial footprint in theater.[6] Whenever access is opposed; infrastructure (airfields, ports, fuel, water, etc.) is lacking; or

---

[5]One example would be a limited raid, such as the August 1998 cruise-missile strikes in Afghanistan and the Sudan after the embassy bombings in Nairobi and Dar es Salaam and the April 1986 air strikes in Libya in response to terrorist actions in Rome, Vienna, and Berlin.

[6]The long-range ballistic missiles, conventional or reusable, have the same allure if they can be distinguished from nuclear weapons. Long-range aircraft and cruise missiles are somewhat less alluring; although they can respond within about a day, they are handicapped by overflight restrictions.

land, sea, or air forces simply are not available, space forces could initiate or support operations. In such a theater, space forces should be the first, or among the first, forces employed. However, unless they themselves are backed up with suitable replenishment logistics, they cannot operate alone for long before sharing some of the burden with other forces arriving in theater. Even if the space forces have the logistical staying power to operate alone for an extended time, it would be better for other forces with complementary strengths to join in as soon as possible. Extended operations by only one kind of force will quickly teach the opponent to adapt to its limitations. Instead, the preference should be to combine complementary forces quickly in a concentrated, joint operation. With these general caveats, the duration of a space-only or space-heavy period of operations would depend on the specifics of the threat and theater and on the reach and speed of the air, land, and naval forces joining the fight.

When air, land, and naval forces do join the fight, they should fill the gaps and relieve some or most of the space force's burden. Aircraft and surface-to-air missiles should be able to prosecute air targets in bad weather that space-based lasers cannot penetrate. As enough assets arrive, they should take over the burden in fair weather where they can reach. As airborne lasers and surface-to-air missiles arrive, they should prosecute ballistic missile targets within their reach, leaving the targets out of reach to the space-based lasers. Aircraft and cruise missiles should be able to attack interdiction targets.

When other forces are in play, the special attributes of space weapons should enter into decisions about when and how to employ them. Because of their quick response, space weapons may be the only ones that can reach fleeting targets in time—provided that the value of the target is worth expending the weapon.

When the risk of using manned aircraft is unacceptable, space weapons could accomplish many strategic attack and interdiction objectives traditionally reserved for the air component. Currently, the low-risk alternatives are to drop precision-, laser- or Global Positioning System–guided bombs from aircraft that are beyond the reach of air-defense artillery (once the surface-to-air missile threat is suppressed), to drop precision bombs from stealthy airplanes (when the threats are not suppressed), or to use cruise missiles. However, even stealthy aircraft are vulnerable to the "golden BB" of random antiaircraft fire. Cruise missiles can be shot down en route to their targets and may be as logistically expensive as space alternatives, depending on how launch platform costs are counted. Opponents may withhold and hide some air defense missiles to prevent suppression.

In hostile air defense environments in which the chance of losing a pilot is high, space weapons could be an alternative to high-altitude aircraft or cruise missiles. For small numbers of heavily defended, high-value targets, space weapons could be the weapon of choice. This may make them particularly attractive for strategic attacks on enemy economic and infrastructure targets, which are often fixed and may be protected. Because the responsiveness of space weapons is high relative to the sortie times and scheduling complexity of long-range stealth bombers,[7] it may be easier to achieve the shock effects of mass and concentration against such targets using space weapons, either alone or in conjunction with the aircraft for restrike after damage assessment. If they are being used for the first time against an opponent, their unfamiliarity might also add to the shock.

Because of the difficulty in defending against space weapons that provide destructive suppression or radio frequency jamming, they may also be helpful in suppressing enemy air defenses at targets that need a heavier air attack. But if the attacks are not suitably synchronized with air operations, they may only alert air defenses. On the other hand, because of the agility and reach of space weapons, this effect might be exploited to misdirect and confuse air defenses.

Given an adequate understanding of targets, conditions, timing, and quantities of space weapons in the context of joint warfare, it should be possible to develop effective concepts for their employment. However, their employment concepts will depend critically on having suitable structures for commanding the weapons, that is, suitable location and apportionment of command authority. This is the topic of the next section.

---

[7]For example, B-2s operating from Missouri have a 30-hour round trip for sorties to Yugoslavia, requiring multiple refuelings for each leg of the trip (Katzaman, 1999; Ricks, 1999).

Before leaving this issue, we should note one important aside. The conventional definition of *theater* must change when space forces are added to the mix. The geographic bounds of the theater must extend to include the space forces. Any side on the receiving end of space forces (weapons or support) will respond where it can be effective against them. In addition to prosecuting the theater campaign, one of the first-order tasks for space weapons will likely be to help protect itself (when terrestrial forces cannot reach in time). An example of this might be a need for space-based conventional weapons to strike ground-based lasers attacking low-orbit satellites. No matter how we might define the theater or apportion command of space forces, the opponent engaged or threatened by them will consider them to be in theater and legitimate targets.

COMMAND

The essence of command is having the authority to allocate limited resources, human or material, among competing needs—and being accountable for the allocations made. Accountability includes the normally conflicting responsibilities for efficient use of the resources and achieving the intended purpose—largely an issue of effectiveness. The art is in selecting the level of command of forces that can be effective—providing adequate insight into likely consequences before deciding and allowing timely implementation of desired effects after deciding—without squandering resources or hoarding them inefficiently. If the level of command is too low (i.e., too narrowly defined in terms of geography or mission), the commander may not be aware of the consequences of use and depletion of the resource at higher levels. If the level is too high (i.e., too remote for timely awareness), the commander may not be aware of unintended consequences of employment in collateral effects and possible conflict with other operations at lower levels. Because the balance between effectiveness and efficiency depends on changing circumstances and priorities, good mechanisms for command should have the flexibility to adjust to such changes at least as dynamically as the changes occur. However, the general form of mechanisms available will depend on the laws and customs of the country or alliance in question. We will explore the particular forms in U.S. law.

There are three practical questions that need to be answered about command of space weapons:

- *What is commanded?* More specifically, what form and quantity of space weapon resources can a commander with operational control task to subordinate commanders who exercise tactical control?

- *How should they be commanded?* In particular, do space weapons have attributes that make commanding them different from commanding terrestrial weapons?

- *Who commands?* Who should exercise operational and tactical control, given the form of allocation of space resources identified in the first two questions?

What Is Commanded

When we discuss command of space weapons, it is important to distinguish command from the operation of equipment or platforms. It is a commonplace that commanders must have some degree of skill and experience at the technical level in operating the equipment under their command. This can both establish the commander's credibility with equipment crews and improve the morale and esprit of subordinates. It should also improve the commander's credibility with his own peers and superiors responsible for other capabilities.

However, in the case of space weapons, this does not necessarily translate to a need for skill and experience in operating satellites. Since the beginning of human activity involving space, there has been little need for human skill—actually, little tolerance of direct human interaction—in operating space equipment. What does require human skill in operating terrestrial and atmospheric weapons and vehicles is largely the design of satellites. Humans normally interact with space systems to

- resolve anomalies in system operation (an engineering or maintenance activity)

- interpret or use the space system's products or effects

- manage or allocate limited resources among competing requirements in the context of environmental constraints.

Skill and experience in the last two activities may be the valuable prerequisites for commanding space weapons.

Another caution in thinking about operations and employment of space capabilities for terrestrial interaction, particularly for space weapons, is that the unit measuring the thing being operated or commanded should seldom be "satellite." First, with the rare exception of satellites in geosynchronous orbit (unlikely for space weapons targeted against the earth), the space resources needing management and direction are those of the elements of an entire constellation that are within reach of the areas being supported. Second, most satellites have multiple payload capabilities, which can be managed to support multiple purposes with some degree of independence. Finally, even within a single payload, function may often be apportioned flexibly among many uses and customers, either simultaneously or time-shared. A single operator may control a constellation of satellites, transmitting instructions and receiving telemetry through a network to maintain its health and monitor its status. However, command of its employment should be measured in terms of the functional capabilities that may be apportioned flexibly among as many uses and users as needed. The identity, location, and organizational affiliation of the operator need have little to do with the allocation of command authority for employing the constellation's capabilities.

For space weapons, what is commanded should be defined in terms of functional forms of apportionment, as opposed to equipment, satellite, or even constellation forms. Given a definition in terms of function or capability rather than hardware, the need to define form and quantity remains. For example, with a space-based laser, lasing time or fuel consumption may define availability for a secondary mission before resupply; setting time windows for secondary missions may reserve kill-rate capacity needed for higher-priority missions when thin spots in the constellation are overhead.

How They Are Commanded

Several factors influence the command of weapons. Those relevant for the distinctive features of space weapons include technical characteristics of responsiveness, effect, flexibility, precision, cost, and communications architecture.

Responsiveness. Because the lead time for delivering a mass-to-target weapon from space can range from tens of minutes to hours, its responsiveness can limit the types of targets missions for which it might be useful. Longer deorbit times mean that mobile ground and air targets are probably too elusive to be worthwhile, unless the space weapon delivers a conventional submunition with appropriate sensing and reach. In contrast, the time from the firing of a directed-energy space weapon to contact is almost instantaneous, and the delay between contact and effect is short.

The level and structure of command of space weapons should be consistent with the timeliness desired and achievable. In missions that require short decision cycles, tactical control of the more-responsive space weapons could reside with the lowest-level commander having control of all forces on the scene contributing to the task. For example, the theater air defense commander might be allocated a portion of a space-based laser constellation's capacity to manage in real time in conjunction with airborne laser, interceptor, and surface-to-air missile defenses in the area. Command over conventional space weapons with delays of a few minutes might pass to a weapon controller overseeing time-critical targets, who can task sorties of aircraft, surface-to-surface missiles, and artillery against them. And the joint air component commander might exercise control over an allocation of kinetic-energy space weapons as part of an air tasking order to air force and naval aircraft and cruise missiles.

Flexibility. Some space weapons, kinetic-energy weapons in particular, have fairly specific effects that are suitable for a relatively narrow range of targets. Others, directed-energy or conventional munitions, could be used more flexibly against a variety of targets and under a range of more or less restrictive rules of engagement.

Lethal use of space weapons may also provide flexible opportunities that require flexible command. Space-based lasers might be useful against aircraft in flight, cruise missiles, and fuel transporters, as well as the ballistic missiles in boost phase that were the primary reason for acquiring the weapons in the first place. Tailoring the weapon's command structure specifically and solely to the ballistic missile targets would waste its flexibility.

Precision. The precision and selectivity of the space weapon, in particular, the amount of collateral damage it is likely to cause, will help determine when and where it can be used and the appropriate levels of command. For example, in an urban battle, a kinetic-energy space weapon might destroy the basement (and all intervening stories) of a multistoried building—and might also do the same to a few of the neighboring buildings, if the cluster of weapons used were dispersed too highly. Generally, space weapons with less-discriminate effects should be constrained by rules of engagement that require higher levels of command authority to release.

Cost. Space weapons having high logistical or opportunity costs may also require higher command authority. Even though there is no inherent limitation, 20-year-old squad leaders do not have the authority to use million-dollar cruise missiles and should also probably not have the authority to commit a space-based weapon. Similarly, because of the opportunity costs inherent in the resupply time involved in restoring used capacity, the National Command Authorities would likely need to review reallocation to any other purpose of any portion of a space-based laser constellation's capacity needed for national missile defense.

Communications. Commanders at the lowest tactical level may not have the communications necessary to use space assets. However, commanding a space asset does not have to mean much more than the ability to communicate a target location and identity, the desired effect, and the time of attack with the authority to be sure it will be engaged within allocated resource limits. Ideally, the commander should also have enough communication connectivity and capacity to confirm receipt of tasking, be advised of tasking consequences, and to commit resources to the task if the consequences are acceptable. This is not necessarily a difficult communication problem, particularly if there are intermediate relays (or a network) between a mobile commander and the space asset.

Who Commands Them

If effective choices have been made about what is commanded and how it is commanded, determining who commands begins with determining the purpose and who is available, controlling what resources, to accomplish that purpose. The purpose is defined by the mission assigned to a commander.

Who is available to command a space weapon may depend on particulars of the stage of conflict in a theater. In the early phases of future contingency operations that are remote from the United States, little to no terrestrial force may actually be present at the outset. In fact, if it is very early in the conflict, the responsible command authority may not have had a chance to designate a responsible task-force authority. If an entire conflict were to be conducted with U.S.-based long-range forces, say the destruction of a country's infrastructure for weapons of mass destruction, space forces could be under central control from the United States. However, if the conflict required halting an invasion force and introducing shorter-range theater forces to expel it, control of the contributing space forces would presumably shift to the command controlling the introduction and use of theater forces.

If a commander of theater forces has tactical control over all assets devoted to a particular mission or function—such as counter-air or strategic attack—he should have similar control over the space assets contributing to the mission in his area of operations. For example, the commander who usually has tactical control over forces for air defense and airspace control is the Joint Force Commander or the Joint Force Air Component Commander. To prevent fratricide and maximize overall counter-air effectiveness, one could argue that all systems intended to counter ballistic and cruise missiles should also be under his control, including space weapons supporting these theater missions. Gaps in the engagement capabilities of fighters or ground-based air-defense assets could be supplemented by space-based weapons. Space weapons could handle a larger share of the missile threat (or the strategic attack of fixed targets) so that air power could concentrate more on close air support and short-range interdiction. Whoever has tactical control of the forces for a particular mission in a given situation should be responsible for matching all the appropriate weapons against the right kinds of targets and resolving conflicts in their concurrent operations. If space weapons are to be synchronized, integrated, and deconflicted with the allocation of other assets devoted to the same mission, one commander should ideally have tactical control over all the assets allocated to that mission.

Chapter Five

HOW MIGHT THE UNITED STATES ACQUIRE SPACE WEAPONS?

This chapter addresses the following questions:

- Under what circumstances might the United States decide to acquire space weapons?

- If that decision is made, how might the transition occur? What sorts of strategies are available, and what are the possible consequences?

The first question presumes a conscious decision to develop and acquire space weapons. Incidental or accidental outcomes might also be possible, in which the U.S. government makes no deliberate decision to develop space weapons, but related technologies and systems developed for commercial or other purposes then become available for or are applied to military operations. We will examine this possibility as well. Assuming a decision, we then turn to its implementation and examine the consequences of implementing it, intended or not.

HOW MIGHT THE UNITED STATES DECIDE?

There are a number of hypothetical ways the United States might decide to acquire space weapons, which this discussion groups into *deliberate* and *incidental* decisions. The primary interest should be in deliberate decisions; however, to avoid being unpleasantly surprised by an incidental decision, we should not lose sight of the possibility.

Deliberate Decisions to Acquire

Several sets of circumstances might lead U.S. decisionmakers, after measured deliberation, to choose to acquire space weapons, including the following:

- to respond to a threat to national security posed by an adversary who is undeterred by other capabilities

- to respond in kind to another nation's acquisition of space weapons, whether ally or adversary

- with another nation or nations, to forestall, control, or influence their independent acquisition of space weapons

- unilaterally, in the absence of a compelling threat, to demonstrate global leadership, protect U.S. and allied economic investments, improve the efficiency and effectiveness of military capability, etc.

Responding to a Threat by an Undeterred Adversary. If there is an adversary who cannot be deterred by other means, a decision to acquire space-based defenses should be understood in the context of stable deterrent relationships with adversaries who can. Space weapons that might change a perception of first-strike stability should be evaluated for their effects on deterrence.

For example, space-based ballistic missile defenses are inherently thin, not capable of rapid reinforcement, and are therefore naturally subject to saturation by concentrated salvos. Such defenses should not threaten stable first-strike nuclear deterrence, if the opponent believes he will retain enough capability after a first strike on his forces to saturate the defense and still inflict the damage he deems necessary for deterrence.[1] This might be the case for a space-based

---

[1]In an otherwise insightful exposition of first-strike stability dependence on transitions in vulnerabilities and defenses, Wilkening and Watman (1986) attributed a first-strike destabilizing effect to mutual deployment of space-based lasers. They based this on a presumption that "speed-of-light weapons" might enable the side that strikes first against an opponent's defenses to destroy the opponent's defense-suppression capability at the same time. While space-based lasers could promptly destroy other nearby space-based defenses, it is not clear that they could remove the opponent's means of defeating space-based defenses, some of which should be inherent in his deterrent force structure or based out of reach. The presumption of advantage in attack-

laser defense and Russia's large nuclear forces. It might not be the case for China's smaller nuclear forces. Similarly, acquisition of space weapons (kinetic or conventional) to strike terrestrial targets with less warning than existing weapons could degrade first-strike stability if they are perceived to hold enough of the opponent's deterrent force at risk. This might be the case for a target state that depends significantly on fixed, land-based missiles for its deterrent, such as China. This calculus of first-strike stability is particularly important in considering the transition phase between no space weapons and space weapons in place.

Assuming the United States considers such issues before turning to space weapons, there is still the adversary who cannot be deterred by other means. Recent governmental discussions have already reflected a consensus in the executive (Cohen, 1999) and legislative branches (Abrams, 1999) about the imminence of the threat of regional failed-state and nonstate threats having potential access to weapons of mass destruction. The response so far focuses on terminal and midcourse defenses based in the continental United States. However, such opponents have access to unsophisticated countermeasures that can saturate these defenses.[2] Consequently, there is some pressure to accelerate the development of space-based defenses that can engage the threats before they can apply countermeasures (Senate Armed Services Committee, 1999a).

In this context, space-based weapons could provide limited, boost-phase ballistic-missile defense over areas terrestrial, maritime, and airborne defenses cannot reach.[3] The qualifier "limited" is necessary

---

ing the opponent's defenses assumes that the initiating side's laser defenses are thick enough after destroying the other's lasers to deny the opponent a deterring response after the first strike. In stable deterrence, each side should presumably have sized its deterrent force to ride out a first strike and still saturate or penetrate defenses, even if they were undepleted by an initial attack on the other's laser defenses. Losing one's own defenses would not change this unless they were critical to the survival of a large enough deterrent force. This would be so only if the deterrent force were vulnerable to the first strike, say, in land-based silos. However, survivable deterrent forces are available to both sides through combinations of mobility and stealth, as well as defense.

[2]Appendix D discusses this assertion and the range of applicability of space-based weapons to counter in more depth.

[3]At the moment, there is no clearly identified undeterred, rogue-state threat to which the United States could not gain access from littoral areas, although some portions of

for space-based defenses to be useful, given their inherent thinness. It is also necessary, as already mentioned, to preserve stable deterrence with states possessing substantial arsenals of weapons of mass destruction whose use the U.S. nuclear capability can deter.

It could be argued that there is some room between these two necessities for a useful defense against limited threats from undeterrable sources. The rationale for this is as follows: It is still possible to defend against the small undeterrable opponent and to protect a stable deterrence relationship with a large, deterrable power if the depth of the defense is limited but stationed far enough forward (overhead) to eliminate "cheap-shot" counters.[4] If the undeterrable opponent can and does acquire enough means to saturate the boost-phase defense, the hope would be that he has enough of value that holding it at risk is a deterrent.

But the question is this: Do we understand the previously undeterrable opponent's values well enough to know what to hold at risk, and how, with a credible deterrent force? Given such an understanding, the challenge in implementation would be to achieve a good balance between defense, deterrence, and arms control among a large (and growing), diverse population of states with dangerous capabilities.

Responding in Kind to Acquisition of Space Weapons by Another Nation, Ally, or Adversary. Even with another nation's precedent, the United States could, as a matter of principle, elect not to acquire space weapons, or some kinds of space weapons, provided that preserving the principle did not sacrifice vital national interests. For example, the United States might choose not to acquire (and might encourage others not to acquire) a space weapon that was initially more cost-effective than terrestrial alternatives if the acquisition could end up endangering a particularly valuable commons in space. For instance, a conscious decision might be made to forgo weapons that, if only by their destruction in a conflict, might create a perma-

---

Iran might be out of reach for some hypothetical missiles, and some central Asian states could be imagined.

[4]If such terrestrial defenses as forward-deployed naval, ground, and air forces can reach the sources of undeterrable cheap shots, this should be more affordable than a space-based defense.

nent debris hazard for certain orbits. Geosynchronous orbits, a unique and irreplaceable orbital locus, would be particularly worthy of a weapon-free designation.

However, if another nation decided to acquire space weapons first, the decisionmaking context for the United States would probably change radically. The question would cease to be whether the United States should acquire these weapons and become how and what kind it should acquire. A U.S. decision to "respond in kind" could have different purposes and outcomes, depending on the other nation, the nature of the U.S. relationship with that nation, and the U.S. understanding of the other nation's intent. Chapter Six will examine ways in which different classes of other nations might acquire space weapons.

A future peer competitor, say a resurgent Russia or an economically mature China, could decide to acquire space weapons for the same types of reasons reviewed here for the United States. For example, if one such state chose to develop space-based missile defenses for reasons parallel to those we have discussed, it would be possible, even rational, for all the peer states concerned to develop and deploy orbital missile defenses separately or in concert to preserve stable deterrence among major competing powers.

However, depending on the political climate of the time, a unilateral peer-state decision to acquire space weapons could affect public opinion and government decisions in the United States out of proportion to the event and could preclude rational dialog between countries. The obvious example of this was the U.S. response to Sputnik. Despite the technical and military insignificance of the event and despite its having been announced well in advance as part of the International Geophysical Year activities, the U.S. public and political response was of stunned surprise and a "crisis in confidence" (Killian, 1977, pp. 2–12).[5] Imagine the effect if the Chinese disclosed a space-weapon program or capability in a climate charac-

---

[5]Both the United States and the Soviet Union were developing ballistic missiles concurrently; both had successfully tested them before Sputnik; and both publicly planned space launches that year. The U.S. tests were of shorter-warning intermediate-range missiles; the Soviet tests were of ICBMs (Emme, 1961). Sputnik was launched on one of the ICBMs already tested and should have been no more militarily significant than the earlier tests and certainly no surprise.

terized by such events as the Chinese government's internal repression in Tiananmen Square, U.S. congressional allegations about widespread Chinese espionage against U.S. space and nuclear-weapon technology (Cox, 1999), and the Chinese government's official claim that an accidental NATO bombing of their embassy in Belgrade was a deliberate act by the United States (Gertz, 1999; Loeb and Mufson, 1999).

If an ally or friend, rather than an adversary or potential adversary, acquired some kind of space weapons, responding in kind might not entail the same measures. Rather, they might also include commercial and economic competitiveness considerations, diplomatic measures to influence the ally, or incentives that would alleviate the problem that led to the acquisition in the first place. For example, if the French made an effort to acquire space weapons to support their *force de frappe*, the United States might pursue both a diplomatic accommodation of interests and a parallel system acquisition. Again, the U.S. response might turn on interpretations of intent and estimates of the consequences of not responding, regardless of whether the other nation's action was directed against the United States.

It is possible that a friendly state could acquire space weapons as a consequence of U.S. investment and technology supplied to that nation before the United States is ready to decide whether to acquire its own. A plausible parallel example would be Israel acquiring national missile defenses (something the United States itself could not do without revisiting the ABM treaty) with U.S. financial support. In such a case, the political situation that made the investment and technology transfers possible in the first place might severely limit U.S. response options.

A country that is neither a peer competitor nor ally acquiring some kind of space weapon capability might not obviously be directing the action against the United States. But the United States could still expect to confront the consequences of the weapons (if not the weapons themselves). A smaller potential state adversary that cannot expect to succeed in a head-on confrontation using nuclear or conventional weapons might still be able to confront the United States effectively by exploiting a perceived U.S. weakness in some other area, such as some aspect of the U.S. force structure. Thus, a limited space-weapon capability acquired ostensibly for other purposes could later be applied, perhaps in concert with political and diplomatic strategies, against U.S. interests. For example, a regional power in the vicinity of the Indian subcontinent might acquire space-based conventional or kinetic weapons in response to local threats, such as the land-based ballistic missiles of a neighboring power, and later find the space weapons convenient for keeping U.S. carriers away from the Indian Ocean should the United States attempt to use its surface navy to project power there.

Acquiring Space Weapons in Concert with Another Nation(s). Depending on the purpose of the weapons and the intentions of the other states, the United States might choose to acquire space weapons jointly with another nation or nations. One obvious motivation would be to forestall the independent acquisition of a capability over which the United States would otherwise have less influence or control. This decision could be a preemptive response to another nation's apparent intent to set the precedent of space weapons in ways that the United States might deem dangerous. The kinds of weapons that the United States might seek to acquire via international collaboration would likely be such more clearly defensive weapons as missile defenses. The kind of control that the United States might want to exert, aside from operational employment decisions, might be to restrict the opportunity for wider use of the weapons by imposing inherent design limitations. For example, the United States might choose to join a multinational acquisition of space-based lasers for missile defense and constrain the selection of wavelength to keep the lasers' effectiveness out of the atmosphere, where the substantial U.S. advantage and investment in air power could be endangered.

Unilaterally Acquiring Space Weapons in Advance of a Compelling Threat. Here, the United States would decide to pursue a unilateral effort to acquire space weapons without a compelling threat or previous precedent to fulfill several purposes or a combination of purposes. This possibility has been articulated in a number of places, including some popular literature projecting the imminent need for space weapons for U.S. national security (Friedman and Friedman, 1998).

Beyond popular literature shaping public opinion, there is an increasing level of official discussion in formal documentation and public statements. The 1997 Air Force vision, Global Engagement, recognizes that U.S. military use of space beyond supporting terrestrial forces will be "driven by national policy, international events, threats . . ." but anticipates that "the nation will expect the Air Force to be prepared to defend U.S. interests in space when necessary" (Fogleman and Widnall, 1997). U.S. Space Command currently projects that there will be weapons in space for use against terrestrial targets within the first two or three decades of the 21st century, some (related to missile defense) driven by perceived threats and some intended as more effective or timely alternatives to terrestrial capabilities (Estes, 1998). The National Space Policy commits the country to a variety of ballistic missile defense efforts that would fit the earlier case of a threat-driven decision. It also directs the Department of Defense to "maintain the capability to execute the [space] mission areas of . . . force application" (National Science and Technology Council, 1996). What might be meant by executing the mission area is not clear, but the policy at least uses a term (without identifying the threat) normally associated with space weapons applied against terrestrial targets. While less than an unambiguous commitment, it hints at future possibilities and provides some cover for the discussion in Air Force and U.S. Space Command planning documents. Most of these official documents have a tone of eventual inevitability without providing a clear picture of a proximate cause for a unilateral decision to acquire.

The notion of space weapons as a central element of the future U.S. national security, in advance of a specific compelling threat is beginning to appear in scientific advice to the Defense Department. The Defense Science Board (1999) recommended that the Department of Defense acquire some of the space-based weapons described in this text as essential capabilities for implementing the Joint Chiefs of Staff Joint Vision 2010 (Bender, 1999; Shalikashvili, 1996).

Although a threat-driven decision seems more urgent, it is conceivable that the United States could decide to acquire space weapons in advance of a specific compelling threat. Such a decision might be made to implement an emerging vision of U.S. national security needs based on maintaining technical advantage over potential adversaries and providing a greater degree of flexibility and reach for increasingly diverse global operations with a decreasing forward base of infrastructure. A widespread, international appreciation of the possibility, utility, and effectiveness of space weapons combined with apprehension of the intentions of other nation to acquire them could produce a turnabout in worldview. Aviation provides a precedent for this: All but two powers at the Second Hague Conference in 1907 refused to ratify the extension of the consensus moratorium on weapons in balloons that had been adopted at the Hague Conference in 1899 (Futrell, 1989, p. 17).

Incidental Decisions to Acquire

All the paths to acquisition above presumed a conscious, deliberate decision process. But what if the necessary components and technologies were developed for other reasons, such as commercial or civil interests, and then adapted to or employed in military applications, perhaps in the press of operational necessity, without extensive public deliberation?

If this situation ever happens, it would be in the future, given the trends in development of commercial space capabilities. The commercial space industry is not likely to develop specific weapon products. Given current trends, the industry is not even likely to contribute substantially to enabling technology or capacity, except perhaps to reduce the price associated with general large-scale enterprises in space (DeKok and Preston, 1999). But one possible trend in commercial space activity could produce effective means of delivering conventional weapons from space.

Any capability to deliver and retrieve large quantities of material economically to and from space could be adapted to emplace and deliver conventional weapons from space. There is no such ability on the horizon in commercial space activity yet. The only going concern in that business, SpaceHab, relies on a free ride from a heavily subsidized and very expensive space shuttle (SpaceHab, 1999).

However, the lack of such a capability is primarily a question of demand. More-economical spaceflight requires some reuse of its expensive elements, which in turn requires increased design margins in reusable elements for durability and reliability. With the already thin margins inherent in the physics of spaceflight, economic recovery of the investment in reuse requires large scale and rate effects.

There are three possible sources for scales and rates large enough to make reusable spaceflight economically feasible.[6]   One of the longest-anticipated (but still seemingly remote) sources is the possibility of a market for materials that can be processed or manufactured only in space. None has emerged, and no likely candidates are on the horizon.

The most-credible current source of high-rate demand for spaceflight in commercial space activity is communications. Recent proposals for large-scale satellite constellations, such as Iridium and Teledesic, prompted several small entrepreneurial activities to propose reusable launch vehicles. However, the pace of development and the financial success of these activities are sensitive to the continuing development of large-scale commercial communication constellations. The financial failure of the Iridium constellation has clouded that future (Leibovich, 1999).

The Space Transportation Association's (STA's) next great hope for high launch and recovery demand is space tourism. STA formed a Space Travel and Tourism division and sponsored a first-annual conference on the development of space tourism in 1999 (STA, 1999). But the association judged that

> There can be no large space tourism business until the unit cost of surface-LEO [low earth orbit] space transportation is reduced and safety increased, by orders of magnitude re [over] today's Shuttle capabilities. (STA, 1999.)

If or when any of these markets creates a viable industry for economical launch and recovery, the step from transport to weapon carrier could range from trivial to modest. Current U.S. Space Command and Air Force Space Command plans outline how such a transition might take place. The payloads for a space operations vehicle and

---

[6]A possible fourth, noncommercial, source of high-rate demand for launch would be a reusable ballistic-missile–like vehicle intended to deliver large quantities of conventional munitions promptly from the continental United States to distant theaters. Such a vehicle is mentioned in Chapter Three and Appendix C.

space maneuver vehicle could include a common aerospace vehicle to deliver conventional munitions from space to earth. However, because the programs depend on congressional appropriations, a decision to develop space weapons through the government path could hardly be incidental or lack substantial scrutiny and deliberation.

ASSUMING A DECISION TO ACQUIRE, HOW MIGHT TRANSITION OCCUR?

This section does not discuss the mechanics of purchasing or the content of programs, since little here singles space weapons out from other procurements. Rather, the purpose here is to outline possible ways to transition to a world with U.S. space weapons, to identify interactions with the decision processes, and to highlight policy issues that should inform any decision before it is taken.

One of the obvious ways in which the transition might interact directly with the decision to acquire space weapons is in the structure of the decision itself. A structural distinction can be drawn between monolithic and incremental decisions and implementations.

Incremental Decision

When there is significant uncertainty in any decision environment, one normal approach is to use an incremental or hedging decision strategy. The normal defense acquisition phases of concept exploration, demonstration and validation, engineering development, production, and deployment are intended to allow incremental decisions and create options (OUSD[A&T], 1999). Given the uncertainties, risks, and decision context, such an approach would be likely in a U.S. decision about acquiring space weapons. It has already surfaced in the technology development for space-based lasers and in congressional interest in a readiness demonstrator flight experiment (Senate Armed Services Committee, 1999a). For decisions and programs like this, a sequence of incremental decisions would be made to

* develop technology
* develop components and subsystems
* test or demonstrate critical aspects of a capability

- deploy a system
- employ the system for various missions.

Those making these incremental decisions can chose a strategic posture that adapts to the evolving environment, shapes the environment proactively, or reserves the right to play later. However, it is seldom recognized that, despite any preference for an adapting or reserving posture, using this strategy for national security purposes inevitably involves a degree of shaping, some of which can distort the apparent value of the options. The shaping occurs in both internal and external environments. In the internal environment, the shaping occurs with the alignment of institutional positions and the development of constituencies for and against program continuation. Having invested substantially in a program, the resulting constituency for program continuation creates some obligation to continue.

In the external environment, the shaping comes from the changed international perception of U.S. intention and capability and from the decisions of other countries about how to respond to those perceptions. For example, a U.S. commitment to midcourse and terminal-area missile defenses would encourage opponents who expect this action to devalue their own missile forces unacceptably to develop missiles with penetration aids and to engage in early deployment of multiple munitions to saturate the defenses. If the United States committed to a space-based laser for boost-phase missile defense, opponents who felt that the laser would unacceptably devalue their forces might

- develop faster-burning missiles to reduce their period of vulnerability or harden the missiles to reduce the laser's capacity
- proliferate the missiles and their launchers to saturate the lasers
- develop antisatellite capabilities against the lasers
- if the laser's wavelength could not penetrate the atmosphere, shift force structure toward cruise missiles.

In response to these measures, the United States might be compelled to change its lasers' wavelength to penetrate deeper into the atmosphere, to develop defenses for the lasers, etc. The challenge for countries evolving their capabilities is to avoid an unstable arms race. Rational decisionmaking; effective communication between the various countries involved; and a balance of military capability, diplomatic action, and arms control might avoid such an arms race. The history of nuclear deterrence and arms control and reduction provides vivid instances both of arms races (e.g., in the development of MIRVs) and of eventually effective coping (SALT and START).

Monolithic Decision

The alternative to incremental decisions and implementation is a monolithic decision and implementation. In the absence of uncertainty and the presence of urgency, this is likely to be the quickest and most efficient path. However, if the situation is not clear, the urgency may proceed quickly and efficiently to an unintended destination. Perhaps the most profound example of this was the Manhattan Project and the subsequent arms races and proliferation of nuclear weapons. A more benign example might be the race to the moon in response to Sputnik. The possibility of this kind of decision and implementation is greater with the external pressure of ongoing conflict (e.g., World War or Cold War) and the fear of unacceptable consequences (e.g., a Nazi superweapon or nuclear missile attack) magnified by surprise (e.g., Sputnik).

If the scope and impact of the capability sought are small enough, a monolithic space weapons decision might not necessarily run the risks identified in the last paragraph. For example, if another country were to develop weapons against U.S. satellites—perhaps ground-based lasers that could quickly decimate critical low-altitude intelligence satellites before a terrestrial weapon could reach them—the United States could choose a space weapon in response. A space-based weapon might be the only timely response to such a threat. The United States might quietly develop a small number of space-based weapons that could destroy the opponent's antisatellite weapons quickly enough to protect most of the targeted satellites once the threat against the satellites was imminent or attacking. In this case, the effect of the space-based weapons might be seen as reasonably limited and stabilizing, if, or once, disclosed. Disclosure might be necessary to strengthen their credibility as a deterrent. There is some possibility that disclosure would not be required for deterrence and even some possibility that employment on a small scale might not require explicit disclosure of the nature or basing of the weapon.

Scope, Sequence, and Visibility of Implementation

Whatever the structure of the decision and implementation, we need to be aware of other significant implementation factors for understanding the transition to space weapons. The discussion here singles out scope and sequence of capability and visibility of implementation. *Scope of capability* does not refer to a particular, absolute level but rather to the general trend of limited or expansive utility. We mentioned circumstances earlier in which the United States might wish to limit the utility of an internationally developed and controlled space-based laser to targets outside the atmosphere. Conversely, for a U.S. development, there is a natural tendency to leverage large investments in one capability to add additional capabilities and constituents. The United States might choose to develop a space-based laser for missile defense and extend its operation as far into the atmosphere as possible to improve its effectiveness against missiles and to add a capability against aircraft and cruise missiles in clear weather. The previous section noted that this issue of scope can have significant interaction with the control of unintended consequences.

Once the question of scope is raised, there is often a question of sequence for the capabilities included in the scope. For example, including the capability to protect the weapon, as well as to employ it against intended targets, raises questions about how to protect partially deployed capabilities. Would the first space-based lasers launched encounter space mines? Should kinetic-energy antisatellite weapon escorts be launched first? Including protection in the scope also raises questions of what ancillary supporting capabilities might be needed for surveillance; threat detection; defense; and resupply, repair, or replenishment and in what sequence they should be deployed. Would the space-based laser require external space surveillance support of possible attacks from above? Should its assigned missions include imaging potentially threatening satellites to identify them for surveillance or other responses? Will the laser's magazine and resupply logistics be adequate for additional missions, when needed? Getting the sequence wrong could invite an arms race.

Visibility is another parameter influencing transition and consequences. This could be taken as a sharp choice between overt and covert acquisition, in which perhaps the only parameter is the timing of a covertly acquired capability's eventual unveiling. Such a choice might have unpleasant consequences as shock and surprise herald the unveiling. The other extreme of transparency could lead to a race between countermeasures and counter-countermeasures. However, a more useful perspective than either extreme would be to treat the degree of visibility and to whom that visibility is afforded as transition elements to be managed in a way that insures against both unpleasant surprise and unstable competition.

Consequences

The preceding paragraphs gave some examples of hypothetical consequences of a few transition strategies. Ideally, there would be no unanticipated consequences and preferably no unintended consequences of an action as significant as the U.S. acquisition of space weapons. Realistically, given the human creativity and imagination of opponents and allies, a complete enumeration of possible consequences is not reasonable. Even so, some further discussion is warranted here—not to seek or even bound enumeration, but to highlight some of the topics peculiar to space weapons and to suggest ways of navigating the possible consequences. The discussion is arranged according to possible sources of consequences.

Opponents. A potential adversary could choose any of a number of responses to U.S. acquisition of space weapons, depending on his assessment of the weapon and the means available to him. He might attempt to deter its use, if he can formulate or acquire a credible deterrent. If he already has a credible nuclear deterrent, he might seek to link use of the U.S. space weapons to his nuclear deterrent. For example, if he became aware or suspected that a U.S. kinetic-energy space weapon was threatening silo-based ICBMs that were a substantial part of his deterrent force, he could announce a launch-on-warning or launch-under-attack policy tied to the status of the space weapons.

The opponent might choose to attack the U.S. space weapons preemptively with physical means, depending on his perception of the vulnerability of the weapon and its threat to his interests. He might choose to avoid providing the weapon useful targets if it has operational limitations that leave him useful alternative force structures (e.g., cruise missiles instead of ballistic missiles). He might choose to harden some targets if he can develop adequate confidence in his understanding of the weapon's limitations (e.g., burying targets vulnerable to kinetic-energy weapons deeper than he believes they can penetrate, adding insulation against lasers to his missiles). He could attempt to saturate defensive space weapons with multiple targets, real and decoy.

Given a U.S. precedent of one kind of space weapon, an opponent might choose to follow suit, but possibly with another kind, one better suited to his perception of U.S. vulnerabilities and to his own technology and doctrine. For example, a small quantity of U.S. "silver bullet" space weapon carriers able to deliver a small number of precision or brilliant weapons over a broad footprint might engender a response of large numbers of lower-technology bulk weapon carriers delivering large numbers of less-brilliant but still-effective submunitions (such as those described in Appendix D) against U.S. interests (possibly as instruments of terror if not of conventional military utility). A U.S. space-based laser for missile defense might legitimize a variety of antisatellite weapons targeted against all U.S. space capabilities. Although U.S. space capabilities that provide military advantage are already legitimate targets in a conflict, an opponent might still threaten an antisatellite response as a reason not to deploy the space-based laser.

Alternatively, an opponent might judge the utility of the weapons to be not worth their cost and cede the high ground of space, instead adopting the moral high ground and a legal strategy to try to use the U.S. decision to fragment support from its allies and to arouse world opinion against U.S. "hegemony."

Allies. Depending on what it saw at risk from the introduction of weapons into space, an ally might be susceptible to a U.S. opponent's attempt to use a U.S. acquisition decision against the alliance relationship. Among other things, an ally might believe that destructive weapons in space would jeopardize its own intelligence space interests, regardless of whether those interests are potential targets or innocent bystanders. Commercial space interests might also appear to be at increased risk from possible orbital debris resulting from conflict in a region of space important to the ally.

If the United States involved its allies adequately in the decision and implementation of the acquisition, allies could conceivably play some substantial role in the acquisition, support, operation, or use of the weapons. In the absence of that involvement, they may well have reason to feel that the acquisition of a significant capability would threaten their vital interests. At the very least, allies that are not adequately involved in the acquisition would find themselves increasingly relegated to second-tier status, increasing the likelihood and degree of disproportionate roles in alliance operations. There has been evidence of concern about this already in the 1999 NATO operations in Kosovo and Serbia (Drozdiak, 1999).

The World. This section does not attempt a complete catalog of the rest of the world's reactions to a U.S. acquisition of space weapons. One nearly certain consequence, however, would alter the world's environment, effectively permanently, and would unavoidably color international perception of the United States. The one fundamental difference between weapons in space and weapons on land, sea, or in the air is that gravity brings the debris from terrestrial weapons and platforms down and generally confines their effects to a limited area. Aside from some persistent effects of some weapons (nuclear radiation or chemical contamination) and pollution from destroyed platforms, salvage is generally feasible if not economical, and the extent of damage is limited if cleanup is not practical. The damage is seen as the regrettable, but unavoidable, consequence of conflict, to be minimized in ideal conditions of war termination.

Dead satellites, on the other hand, do not fall out of the sky unless they are carefully pushed with considerable effort. If they are fragmented by a violent death, the fragments are not confined to the limited vicinity of the satellite's original orbit. The fragments spread under orbital perturbations around the ring of the orbit they began from and gradually around a shell of orbits near the original orbit (Johnson, 1989, fig. 30, p. 67). Their velocity and mass can make them a hazard to navigation or operation within that shell. Except at quite low altitudes,[7] space debris persists indefinitely.

---

[7]That is, below an altitude of 500 km; even then, there are generational time scales that depend on the extent of solar storm activity heating and raising the upper atmosphere.

Even if a satellite does not die a violent, fragmenting death, any significant stored energy in chemical propellants, batteries, or mechanical energy storage may cause a violent fragmentation after an otherwise peaceful death. Experience has taught satellite and launch vehicle designers and operators to make them completely inert at the end of their useful lives (Committee on Space Debris, 1995).

Choosing to station weapons in space may invite attacks on them that would result in a permanent increase in the space debris hazard, which can be estimated but must be valued in several currencies. From the perspective of space weapons, it may be only a matter of small degree in operational concern and design requirements for maneuver and shielding. From the perspectives of civil, commercial, international law, and the public, the risk may be seen or portrayed as unnecessary,[8] an unwarranted cost, illegal environmental modification,[9] or defilement of principle. The principle defiled is the principle that space is a commons, the "province of all mankind" defined in the Outer Space Treaty: "space . . . shall be free for exploration and use by all . . . not subject to national appropriation by claim of sovereignty" and requiring its use "for the benefit and in the interests of all countries" (UN, 1967).

If the United States is the first to station weapons in space and if the debris hazard in a region of space increases as a result, the world will see the risk as a U.S. choice. Even if the risk is insignificant in actuarial terms, the political consequences may not be.

---

[8]The Liability Convention provides for claims against the launching state for damages caused in orbit if the launching state is negligent. In the case of damage from debris generated by hostile destruction of a satellite, the state that launched the destroyed satellite should not be liable.

[9]The Environmental Modification Treaty prohibits creation in space of "widespread, long-lasting or severe effects as the means of destruction, damage or injury to any other State Party" through the "deliberate manipulation of natural processes" (UN, 1977). There might be argument over whether creating space debris constitutes manipulation of natural processes, but the treaty's stipulation that the effects be widespread and long-lasting definitely applies.

Chapter Six

HOW MIGHT OTHERS ACQUIRE SPACE WEAPONS?

The previous chapter looked at ways the United States could come to a decision to acquire space-based weapons for use against terrestrial targets. Two of these ways depended on another nation's decision to acquire space weapons. Depending on the nature of the other nation and its decision, the U.S. alternatives and response could be very different. How might other nations decide to acquire their own space weapons?

The United States is not the only nation with the opportunity to acquire space weapons. The only option that is proprietary to the United States—lethal directed-energy weapons—is so simply as a consequence of the current state of technology. Given the opportunity for independent choice, why would another country choose? How would it decide? This chapter address these questions from the following perspectives:

- peer competitors
- friends and allies of the United States
- non–peer competitors of the United States
- countries that are neither friend nor foe
- a nonstate coalition of entities (possibly state assisted).

National interests that might motivate interest in space-based weapons are tabulated in Table 6.1.

Individual countries may not fall completely into one of the above categories. So, any country, region, or cause named in this chapter is

Table 6.1

**National Interests of Other Countries That Could Lead
Them to Consider Space-Based Weapons**

Category	National Interest
Security	Limited threats suitable to inherently thin space defenses
	Distant threats needing long-range force projection
	Nearby threats to homeland-based deterrent forces, where longer warning, increased survival, and decreased collateral damage would result from basing deterrent in space (spacefaring alternative to submarine-launched ballistic missiles)
	Balancing or bypassing a competitor's military strengths, such as its navy
Economic	Access to distant resources
Political	Prestige of peer recognition, global reach
	Independence from U.S. capabilities
	National survival
	Freedom from external interference in internal or regional affairs
	Promotion or protection of beliefs, values, system of government

used purely for illustration. The discussions here therefore do not represent any judgments about these entities or their intentions but rather are simply abstractions of a particular attribute of or similarity to the perspective under discussion. None of this discussion is meant to suggest imminent decisions by any of the countries or to malign any area or cause.

PEER COMPETITOR

Throughout the Cold War, the United States had only one peer competitor: the Soviet Union. In a military sense, the United States has no peer competitors at the moment. That may change, and the military sense is not the only sense of competition that matters for a decision to acquire space weapons. A peer might decide to acquire them to reduce or bypass U.S. military advantages. An economic competitor might decide to acquire them to gain an independent ability to protect its own global interests, not because of a desire for a confrontation with the United States.

Although it might be natural to think of future peers in the same terms once used of the Soviet Union, that would be too narrow here. The previous chapter named a resurgent Russia or an economically mature China as potential examples of a future peer competitor. By another definition, a politically cohesive European Union might also become a peer competitor. Therefore, discerning a nation's motivations and its interests in space weapons and clarifying the range of U.S. concerns and consequences require a careful definition of the term *peer competitor.*

Definition

First, let us define *peer* in the context of national capabilities and interests. *Capabilities* include both technical abilities (technology and resources, including geographic) and economic resources. In the realm of technical abilities, a peer competitor should be defined in terms of the ability to acquire any of the kinds of space weapons considered here that are of possible interest to the United States.[1] This includes an expectation that a peer competitor would have its own means of access to space.

In the realm of economic strength, a peer competitor need not have the same economic resources and capacity as the United States but should be able to devote economic resources to national security on a scale large enough to achieve goals similar to those of the United States. Size clearly matters but should not be measured too precisely or against the same standards that would apply to the United States. Other nations might be able to spend a higher percentage of their overall economy on space weapons, if the decision process and priorities allowed. Others might also acquire similar capabilities with less actual outlay than the United States would for a similar problem—if the development processes and standards allowed greater efficiency or failed to capture some of the external costs (such as environmental costs). The definition of *peer* in this case depends on the kinds and scale of military capabilities achievable, not necessarily on being a true economic peer.

---

[1] Although the levels of technology or technical approaches and styles might be different.

Peer might also be defined in terms of similarity in the kinds of national interests that would make a space weapon attractive. For example, just as developing Korean capabilities spurred U.S. interest in a limited national missile defense against accidental or small, rogue-nation attack, Indian capabilities might spur Chinese interest in such defenses. In a more general example, a peer in motivation would be a country with interests that require the possibility of global, or at least long-range, force projection. In this case, the peer's military capabilities need not match those of the United States. The peer's interest in space weapons would likely be greater if it did *not* have an existing investment (financial and institutional) in a long-range navy or air force. Among the other national interests that might define a peer competitor is a desire to be seen as a peer of the United States in technology and influence.

Decision

Any of the four circumstances that might lead to a U.S. decision to acquire space weapons—responding to an undeterred threat, responding in kind to another's acquisition, joint acquisition to forestall or control, and unilateral acquisition in advance of a compelling threat—might likewise apply to a peer competitor. As noted in the previous chapter, the first circumstance might lead the United States and a peer to cooperate in a form of the third circumstance. A U.S. decision to acquire unilaterally would almost certainly lead a peer to the second circumstance. The circumstance of greatest interest to the United States is the fourth: unilateral, unforced acquisition.

Several of the national interests listed in Table 6.1 could motivate a decision to acquire space weapons in the absence of a direct threat. Two common threads run through them all: reach and autonomy.[2] Given the global nature of U.S. interests, reach is almost certain to be tangled up with U.S. interests. But such an entanglement could become an opportunity for cooperation if the U.S. role in that cooperation did not threaten the other nation's autonomy.

---

[2]Particularly autonomy from the United States.

One security interest in Table 6.1 was the protection of deterrent forces. Space basing does not automatically improve the survivability of a deterrent. Improvement depends on the terrestrial alternatives available to the country and on the threats available to its opponents. Basing a deterrent force of weapons of mass destruction in space would create a new arena of competition between stealth and surveillance similar to that of submarines but without a hard limit on depth and volume. Deep basing of satellite weapons with deterrent response times on the order of days would create a very large volume for hiding and searching. Stationing a deterrent in space for greater security would almost certainly include a prerequisite decision to withdraw from, abrogate, or ignore the Outer Space Treaty, unless the deterrent were not a weapon of mass destruction. Abandoning the precedent of that treaty might seem a large step for a peer to contemplate, given the international condemnation one would expect to follow. However, the response might not be as severe a deterrent as one might hope. In 1966 and 1967, the Soviets tested a fractional orbit nuclear bombardment satellite to the point of operational readiness after signing the treaty.

Transition

The transition issues for a peer competitor parallel those for the United States. The best circumstances (from a U.S. perspective) occur when the peer adopts an incremental and visible decision and transition. Under those circumstances, there is greater chance for the competitors to avoid an unstable arms race. Idealistically, they might be able to find ways to implement a cooperative, even multinational, solution that might constrain subsequent activity by other countries. More realistically, they might be able to combine weapon development and arms control for mutually stable national security—if there is adequate mutual visibility and shared concern for the costs and consequences of competition.

Where the peer's transition might differ from one for the United States would be in its decision processes and its national interests. Under a different political system, the decision process might be generally less visible. A less visible transition strategy would mean that the U.S. intelligence community would find discerning intention and capabilities from observable indications more challenging and expensive. There would be greater likelihood of surprise and, with it, greater likelihood of an arms race.

Reconciling differing national interests presents two challenges. The first is discerning the peer competitor's interests clearly, but increasing dialogue between the peers should improve this. The second challenge is more problematic. Many of the political interests cataloged above were phrased in terms of autonomy. Some of the national-security interests were phrased in terms of countering the United States. Accommodating the peer's political interests in autonomy would limit the possibility for cooperative deployment of space weapons. Adjusting to efforts to counter U.S. capabilities with space weapons would inevitably require some changes to the U.S. force structure and possibly to the national strategy. If the peer's space weapons could deny U.S. surface vessels access,[3] both the U.S. force structure and the U.S. posture for forward deployment and basing of all forces would have to change substantially if U.S. strategic aims did not change.

FRIEND OR ALLY

The previous chapter mentioned the possibility that a friendly state might be able to acquire space weapons thanks to U.S. investment and technology or because of its own developments, even if the United States has not made the decision to acquire them. Israel's acquisition of missile defenses would be a precedent. To explore motivations for an ally's or friend's decision to acquire space weapons, we will focus on a few examples that are as more or less plausible, such as the Israeli example, and will mention others. Again, this discussion is hypothetical and is not intended to impute real motives or the possibility of such a decision to any of the examples.

---

[3]A recent article in the *Naval Institute Proceedings* pointed out that orbiting antiship weapons might make U.S. carriers obsolete (Roy, 1997). However, the author judged the prospect as a long-term concern because of the difficulty, magnitude, and availability of the launch capability needed to deploy such weapons.

Definition

The defining attribute of the set of friendly or allied nations we consider here is that strong common interests have established a mutual relationship, either formalized by treaty or established over time by custom.[4] Since the United States would not perceive these countries as threats to its interests, their decision to acquire space weapons would not evoke the adversarial response a competitor's decision might. The reason to consider this group separately is precisely that the United States would perceive their actions differently and would choose from a different set of responses. The mutual relationship frequently includes a security element, but need not. Friends or allies include any of the NATO members, Australia, Israel, Saudi Arabia (or one of the other Gulf States that share U.S. interests in regional stability and security), Japan, South Korea, and Taiwan. Considering which of these might have the means to acquire what kind of space weapons narrows the set further.

Capability

The first prerequisite for these weapons is access to space. Among the candidates here, France, Japan, and Israel have indigenous space-launch capabilities. Russian and possibly U.S. firms may soon be launching from Australia, conceivably giving it the capability to launch space weapons without interference, at least if not detected. Taiwan has offered financing for the Kistler reusable space launch vehicle in exchange for a commitment to transfer the technology when it is mature (Barensky, 1999). Others might be able to do something similar; might license an indigenous space-launch capability; or might purchase launches from Russia, Ukraine, China, India, France, or the United States, if they could conceal their purpose.

The second prerequisite for acquiring space weapons is satellite technology. France, the United Kingdom, Germany, Italy, Japan, and Israel already have adequate satellite industries and technology for

---

[4]The only distinction we draw here between friend and ally is the existence of formal agreement for the ally. The common attribute we rely on here is the close relationship with the United States.

the development of some kinds of space weapons. Those with ICBMs and reentry vehicles of their own design (France, U.K.) already have the technical basis for developing mass-to-target space weapons. As Chapter Three noted, this technology is not especially difficult or inaccessible. If (or when) international markets develop for reusable space systems and recovery of material from orbit, the capability to acquire mass-to-target space weapons should become commonplace among all these satellite-building countries and possibly others. Technology for targeting directed-energy weapons in space against terrestrial targets should remain quite rare (except for nondestructive energy levels and long—that is, radio—wavelengths), although within reach of many of these countries should they find the incentive to invest enough resources to develop it.

The final prerequisite for the capability to acquire space weapons is resources. Except for the substantial initial investment needed to develop a space industry from scratch or to develop space-based directed-energy weapons with power and size great enough to cause damage on the earth, this is a matter of degree. If the need is for immediate response, global reach, and many targets, the resources needed would be large. However, if the urgency, coverage, and quantities are relaxed, the resources could fit within national security budgets for many of these countries.

Decision

Of the four circumstances listed for acquiring space weapons noted for the United States, the first and fourth may be the most plausible for friends and allies. The first circumstance, acquisition of space weapons in response to an undeterred threat, is understandable given the political interest of national survival in the face of a nearby threat. This would be particularly understandable if the threat's proximity could undermine the credibility of our friend's homeland-based deterrent. A small country may have little area in which or opportunity to hide a mobile deterrent and may lack confidence in a deeply buried deterrent. The country might also have no ready access to an ocean or may lack the naval infrastructure to protect and hide a deterrent at sea.

Israel and Taiwan face this kind of threat; Israel's is closer, but Taiwan's is larger and nuclear. South Korea could face this kind of threat if North Korea acquires suitable weapons. Of these three, only Israel, at the moment, is reputed to have a nuclear deterrent (Cohen, 1998). When facing similar concerns about vulnerable deterrents, the other nuclear powers chose to develop submarines armed with nuclear missiles. Most already had the underlying naval and ship-building infrastructure. For Israel, developing such an infrastructure would likely be a larger undertaking than was the nation's current satellite and space launch capability development. A space-based nuclear deterrent could be more attractive, particularly given Israel's modest defense budget ($6.5 billion in 1995) and already large share (10 percent) of gross domestic product spent for defense (CIA, 1996).

The issue is less urgent for the fourth circumstance, acquisition of space weapons in advance of a compelling threat. Nevertheless, a decision motivated by critical economic interests in maritime trade and access to distant resources would be understandable, particularly if combined with some other constraints on more conventional maritime power projection.

Transition

While the greatest concern with a peer competitor's transition to owning space weapons is avoiding an arms race, it would not be with a friend or ally. A more likely concern for the United States here would be the setting of a precedent and wider application of the precedent. The transparency of the decision and transition is as critical an issue with an ally or friend as it is with a peer competitor. The difference is the range of possible responses.

For example, both the decision to acquire a space-based maritime patrol force for out-of-area reach and the transition to it would be fairly transparent. Given early insight into a friend or ally's intent to acquire such a force, the United States should be able to offer the friend assistance that could make the space force unnecessary, at least as long as the United States maintains the global reach of its conventional maritime forces. While this might not, at worst, dissuade the friend or ally entirely, it might achieve some degree of control or influence by joining or assisting the friend in acquisition of the capability.

In another example, a small country with neighboring enemies and little room for a terrestrial deterrent might not be so transparent. Israel has relied more on ambiguity than overtly demonstrated credibility for its reputed nuclear deterrent.

NEITHER ALLY NOR ADVERSARY

Definition

Clearly, many states are neither peer competitors nor friends or allies. These states do not generally have the range of global interests that might motivate a preference for space weapons but may have regional security concerns that could provide the motivation. The Indian subcontinent, for example, is one possible locus for interest in space weapons, with possibly unpleasant consequences for the United States. While these neither-friend-nor-foe states may not be adversaries of the United States, their acquisition of space weapons might increase the possibility of bringing them into conflict with the United States. The fact that these are neither friends nor allies limits the range of possible U.S. responses to a decision one of them might make to acquire space weapons. Similarly, because such nations do not have the capacity to threaten that a peer competitor would have, the United States might have more possible responses than it would with a peer.

Capability

Some of these countries, such as India, have their own access to space. Others might acquire it in the manner described for friends or allies, although access might be more difficult because of missile technology proliferation controls. However, these controls have proven to be porous. Some, such as Pakistan, have already acquired the beginnings of launch technology by buying missiles from North Korean. Others, such as Brazil, have had their own indigenous space launch developments, at times with assistance from the United States, Russia, or China.

Of these sample countries, only India has a well-developed indigenous satellite industry, the second prerequisite for these weapons. None of them has needed ICBMs, but the technology for reentry from orbital velocities is reasonably within reach of any of these nations. Should commercial reusable space systems become commodities, mass-to-target weapons on some limited scale could become within reach even of smaller countries, much as small states maintain state airlines with small fleets. The technology for targeting space-based directed-energy weapons against terrestrial targets should remain beyond the reach of most countries that might fall in this group, unless the technology is acquired in cooperation with a peer competitor of the United States. Finally, these countries have sufficient resources for a limited arsenal of space weapons.

Decision

Of the four circumstances for acquiring space weapons, the first (acquisition of space weapons in response to an undeterred threat) seems the most likely for a state that is neither friend nor foe. For example, it might be reasonably plausible for either Pakistan or India to find itself in a position something like Israel's in the last section.

The second circumstance (responding in kind to another's acquisition) is possible and is, in fact, likely if the other nation is a regional competitor. However, in this situation, the implicit question is "which came first, the chicken or the egg?"

In the third circumstance (acquisition with another country), however, the intent might not necessarily be to forestall or control. Rather, the intent would more likely be to achieve a capability sooner or to achieve one greater than would be possible alone.

Transition

The United States might be concerned about the precedent a country that is neither friend nor foe would set by being the first to acquire space weapons. Rather than being concerned that the country would immediately use these weapons to compete with a regional power, the United States should be concerned that the regional power might become a more aggressive international actor—more inclined to intervene where the United States has interests or to exclude the United States from areas of interest. The country's interests might expand to match the more global scope that the longer reach of its new weapons would provide. The Indian subcontinent provides an example. India might use the conventional space weapons it developed for Pakistani nuclear missile targets to try to make the Indian Ocean its own (at least for surface navies). India might threaten U.S. aircraft carriers it thought might interfere with something it considered a local matter, say, intervention in Sri Lanka's Tamil insurrection. Taking the example a little further, India might extend its concern to air forces operating from Diego Garcia and threaten the base itself.[5]

If a country that is neither friend nor foe decided to acquire space weapons, the United States might offer friendly assistance with the proximate cause for the decision. However, with no suitable, established relationship between the countries, such an offer might be suspect. Alternatively, the United States might employ some of the approaches discussed for a peer competitor, but that runs a risk of, in effect, creating another peer competitor. Such a possibility might actually become an incentive for acquiring such weapons—a poor man's path to major-power status, achieving global reach without the expense of a navy or air force capable of competing with the U.S. Navy or Air Force. For such a country, if engagement failed to prevent a decision and if U.S. assistance with the proximate cause were not welcome, the best response might be international, possibly including a space arms control regime.

NONPEER ADVERSARY

The earlier discussion of competitors neglected such smaller, less-capable, or more-isolated countries as North Korea, Iran, and Iraq, which might be considered adversaries. Such countries have limited ability to acquire space weapons independently.[6] Were reusable space systems to become readily available commodity items, modest

---

[5]India does not need to acquire space weapons to pursue regional sea control. It has been acquiring Russian submarine and missile technology that could be used for the purpose, but these weapons are precisely the threat that U.S. naval forces evolved to defeat over the course of the Cold War (Ahmedulla, 2000).

[6]Although, given North Korea's surprise on multistage ballistic missiles and a satellite launch, the United States should not be too complacent about its ability to field some kind of space weapon—particularly with the kind of nontraditional approach outlined in Appendix D.

trade and nonproliferation controls would make acquiring such systems difficult for an isolated adversary. However, the difficulty is that a nonpeer adversary may not be a universal pariah. Indeed, in a major peer competition, a smaller adversary might become a client state of a U.S. peer competitor or at the very least a customer for the elements of space weapons.

The first circumstance (response to an undeterrable threat) seems the most likely here, with the United States perceived as the threat.[7] As with a nonaligned country, the third circumstance (acquisition in concert with others), modified slightly for acquisition in concert with a peer competitor or other adversary of the United States, might be plausible here. Acquisition in concert with another country would almost certainly not be with intent to forestall or control but to achieve a capability it could not manage alone. The second circumstance (response in kind) is possible in response to a U.S. precedent but would likely yield a very asymmetrical capability.

Included here are countries the United States has referred to as *rogue states* (now referred to as *states of concern*)—states acting outside the international community. The decision process and transition would almost certainly not be transparent to the United States. The worries here go well beyond setting precedents, and an arms race is not an issue. The significant concern here is the likely willingness of one of these states to use any space weapons it might acquire particularly if they are weapons of mass destruction. As Appendix D points out, the possibility is not restricted to high-technology, advanced industrial countries.

With a rogue state, the United States should be most concerned with the allure of a poor man's path to major power reach. If engagement fails to convert such a country from adversary to friendly (or at least to nonaligned) status and if nonproliferation controls fail, the only remaining alternatives are intrusive international intervention, as with Iraq's weapons of mass destruction after the Gulf War; preemptive unilateral action; or preparation for conflict in space.

---

[7]The United States, of course, might consider this particular situation to fall under the fourth circumstance: unilateral, unforced acquisition.

NONSTATE COALITION

The final class of actor that might be able to put weapons in space for terrestrial use at some point is not a country, but a coalition of actors (perhaps including states or failed states). One example is the transnational terrorist activity associated with Osama bin Laden. It is not obvious that space weapons would be more attractive than truck bombs to such an entity. But it was also not obvious that Aum Shinri Kyo would be able to develop chemical weapons. Another group might pay more attention to effective means of delivery than Aum Shinri Kyo did in its relatively ineffective release of sarin in the Tokyo subway system. If incidental development via commercial, reusable space systems is taken into account, the difference between a truck bomb and a space cargo recovery module bomb might be only a question of time and selection of suitable ordnance.

The obvious circumstance for such a coalition actor to consider space weapons is to defeat its perceived threat. The other circumstances seem relevant only to nation-states. However, this case implicitly exploits capabilities, such as space launch, resulting from the endeavors of nation-states or their commercial industries. Such a group is, by definition, criminal because it uses violence and is not a state. The U.S. concern is not with precedent or competition but the criminal act. So, as with the rogue states, the alternatives are intrusive international intervention, preemptive unilateral action,[8] and preparation for conflict. To the degree that this activity is criminal and is embedded in ordinary commerce, the United states would prefer to use police and intelligence services, rather than the military, to deal with such entities. However, for some time to come, it is likely that only the military would have the means for surveillance, inspection, and interdiction in space—and only if it recognizes the threat.

SUMMARY

The option for any country to acquire space weapons is not about to expire. Only the option to acquire lethal, directed-energy weapons is proprietary to the United States, and this advantage is neither inher-

---

[8]Neither has been effective so far with such terrorists as Osama bin Laden.

ent nor indefinite, but merely a consequence of the current state of technology.

There is no immediately compelling threat driving any country to acquire space weapons, unless it is the overwhelming advantage in terrestrial weapons that the United States enjoys. Any country's decision to acquire them could be made incrementally to gather information on cost, utility, and competitive response from other countries. A country's ability to acquire them monolithically and covertly should be a concern for the United States.

Earlier chapters pointed out the consequences for U.S. national security strategy of another nation acquiring space-based weapons that could deny maritime access. This chapter points out that these weapons are reasonably within reach of many countries and that they could be developed covertly, disguised in satellite and ballistic missile programs.

Chapter Seven

CONCLUSION

The primary purpose of this report is to provide a common vocabulary and a common set of expectations for the discussion of space-based weapons. The capabilities of such weapons are similar to those of weapons based on terrestrial and atmospheric platforms, differing somewhat in degree and suffering some inherent constraints. Space basing could grant some advantages in access, reach, and promptness in exchange for increased logistic expense and limited ability to concentrate (particularly for defense) or penetrate (earth, water, or weather).

ADVANTAGES

Orbital basing of some kinds of weapons seems to have a number of advantages (although some of these may actually be two-edged swords).

Access and Reach

Here, *access* means access to a target without political constraints on overflight or passage of the platform carrying the weapon, and *reach* refers to the ability to engage a broader, perhaps global, range of targets than other weapons can. Space weapons share these attributes to a degree with ICBMs. Space weapons generally have global reach, although some weapons can reach into the northern or southern hemisphere using roughly half the weapons needed for global reach. ICBMs have roughly hemispheric reach. If there is some concern about limiting the countries that might feel threatened by a space weapon, reach could be a liability. Within a budget for the number and size of weapons and platforms, reach and responsiveness will be trade-offs.

Responsiveness

Even with relatively few space weapons and platforms, the time it takes to have one in position to attack a particular target will be less than the time needed for most terrestrial weapons—unless the terrestrial weapons have already been deployed to the theater of operations containing the target. It could take a few hours for a space-based kinetic-energy weapon to strike its target after release, given weapon logistics comparable to those of terrestrial alternatives. It could take about 20 minutes after release for a space-based conventional weapon to be deployed in the vicinity of a surface target. In contrast, it takes a few days to some weeks for terrestrial weapons to reach a theater of operations from the United States. Long-range ballistic missiles, which reach their targets in times comparable with space weapons, are the exception. However, long-range ballistic missiles are strongly associated with weapons of mass destruction.

The responsiveness of space-based weapons may also be seen as a disadvantage. When the objective of owning weapons of mass destruction is to deter others who have weapons of mass destruction, shorter times make stable deterrence more difficult if they threaten the survivability of the opponent's deterrent. Some have suggested that the timeliness of ground attack weapons from space would threaten the stability of nuclear deterrence. But this is not necessarily so. Because the deorbit times for practical space-based weapons are at best comparable with and generally longer than those of existing ballistic missiles, short warning times would degrade deterrence only if surveillance systems were unable to see space weapons deorbit and if the terrestrial nuclear deterrent forces were vulnerable to the space weapons. Surveillance of space for reliable attack warning is more difficult than surveillance of the earth for missile warning, but it is possible from space. However, warning of an attack is not absolutely necessary for preserving stable deterrence if enough of the opponent's deterrent forces are survivable. Among terrestrial nuclear deterrent forces, only stationary or slow-moving surface platforms, such as silo-based missiles, would be vulnerable to a first strike from space. But thanks to accurate ballistic missiles, silo-based missiles have been vulnerable for a long time, so most nuclear deterrent forces are at least partially based on mobile launchers or submarines to improve survivability. These measures are just as effective against space-based threats.

Distance

Distance from other weapons and basing modes may help to distinguish a space-based weapon from another kind. For example, space-based kinetic or conventional weapons that might be more economically based on terrestrial ballistic missiles could be usefully differentiated from nuclear weapons normally based on terrestrial ballistic missiles, if others were confident that the space platforms did not carry weapons of mass destruction. The great distance from other things that is normal in space can improve the survivability of space-based weapons. There is also a downside to distance. If the space-based weapons were weapons of mass destruction, their physical distance from other targets might make stable deterrence more difficult by inviting a disarming first strike with less collateral damage. Also, distance and gravity are the sources of the logistic limitations we will see in the next section.

Difficulty of Defending Against Them

Finally, some kinds of space-based weapons for some kinds of targets can be extremely difficult to defend against or defeat. The leading example of this is kinetic-energy weapons against fixed or slowly moving surface targets. The difficulty of defending against them results from the weapons' very high velocity and very brief flight through the atmosphere. The difficulty is similar to that of defeating ICBM reentry vehicles.

LIMITATIONS

On the other hand, basing some kinds of weapons in space also has some apparent disadvantages (some of which may also be two-edged swords).

Static Defense

Because achieving a particular orbit requires such enormous effort, significantly changing established orbits is not generally practical. As a result, it is hard to concentrate the efforts of a constellation of satellites in space and time. As defenses, space weapons are static in the same way that terrestrial fortifications are. Space-based defenses are inherently subject to saturation by a terrestrial opponent that is able to concentrate an attack against them in space and time. This limitation may be an advantage if a limited defense against a limited threat is needed that is observably incapable of destabilizing a deterrence relationship with another, larger threat.

Stable, Observable, Predictable Orbits

Although the distances involved and the opportunity for activity to take place out of the view of a particular part of the world may make surveillance and observation of satellites difficult, it is hard to prevent someone willing to spend the necessary resources from observing satellites. Because orbits are subject to only minor unpredictable disturbances, satellite positions are predictable. If the satellites are defenses, the depth of the static defense they provide will vary over the course of their orbits. And because orbits are stable and predictable, the variation in defense depth will be predictable and exploitable. Another downside to stable orbits is that a satellite destroyed in orbit leaves behind a persistent debris field that increases the hazard to other satellites needing to transit its orbit.

Logistic Expense

Launching objects into space is notoriously expensive on both a per pound and a per launch basis. Placing weapons in space should be expensive for the same reasons. Orbiting and deorbiting weapons will always require a greater effort than launching one on a ballistic trajectory. The extra effort is roughly equivalent to that needed to launch the long-range missile's weapon again, but this time at medium range. However, neither the absolute cost per pound of transporting space weapons nor the effort relative to that for missile weapons is a complete enough comparison of space and terrestrial weapon logistics to establish a clear-cut preference.

Terrestrially based weapons have to be flown or shipped into the theater in which their targets are located. Because it is hard to determine how much of the related costs—in terms of transportation infrastructure and delivery force structure—would be saved by space basing, it is difficult compare the costs of the two alternatives.

However, delivering space-based weapons to a theater target would require expending fuel to the tune of some 50 times the weapon's weight, as opposed to a reported 40 times the weight for an air-delivered theater weapon.[1] Operational considerations or the costs of acquiring and owning the necessary infrastructure might outweigh the difference, depending on a country's existing relevant capabilities. A country with a long-range navy and air force would have less reason to be interested in space weapons. A country without such forces might find acquiring space based alternatives economical for some purposes.

The logistic expense for delivering and sustaining space-based weapons that do not deliver mass to their targets is still substantial. The delivery expense is the cost of launching some number of very large satellites. The cost of sustaining expendables will vary with the energy consumed in operation. A representative conceptual design for a space-based laser to defend against ballistic missiles would consume fuel weighing as much as a small satellite for each missile killed.

For a complete picture of the logistic expenses of space-based weapons, multiply the transportation costs for a single space-based weapon by the number of weapons required to cope with absenteeism.

Large Numbers

A corollary of the significant effort required to establish or modify an orbit is that it generally takes a constellation of satellites in orbit to ensure that one will be within reach of an area of interest when you want it to be. The number required to have one in the right place when needed is the absentee ratio. Naturally, if there is something

---

[1]See the discussion of Table B.5 in Appendix B.

useful for the absentees to do when they are out of reach of one task, they are not entirely absentees. When they are useful globally all the time, they are not absentees at all. This is normally not the case for weapons, although it frequently is for reconnaissance, communications, or surveillance satellites. Space weapons for striking targets on earth can have absentee ratios on the order of three to six, roughly comparable with terrestrial weapons, yielding a level of responsiveness that is competitive with that of in-theater and much better than that of out-of-theater terrestrial weapons. In contrast, the timeliness needed for space-based ballistic missile defense requires absentee ratios measured in dozens.

Legal Consequences

Existing treaty provisions limit U.S. space weapons, explicitly restricting the basing of missile defenses or weapons of mass destruction in space. A decision to base missile defenses in space would require changing or abandoning the ABM treaty and, probably, the associated arms control treaties as well. There is also a difference in liability for use of space weapons against the earth that could make a user liable for terrestrial damage the weapon may cause, unless the use and subsequent damage resulted from actions the claimant state had taken with the intent to cause damage (which should be the case for weapons used in legitimate self-defense).

USES AND IMPLICATIONS

Space-based weapons may have a few unique and some useful niches in terrestrial conflict. They might compete well with some terrestrial basing alternatives for some tasks, depending on a country's investment in alternatives and their continuing costs. Useful niches might include prompt, long-range force projection; strikes on highly defended surface targets; and strikes on large surface vessels. Unique niches might include denied-area boost-phase missile defense and prompt destruction of terrestrial antisatellite weapons.

Regardless of the nation acquiring them, space-based weapons could change the logistics and responsiveness of long-distance military activities and would shift the proportion of forces and assignment of tasks between long-range and short-range forces somewhat.

Although these weapons would not make shorter-range weapons or major military force components (army, naval, air force) obsolete, they could make some systems or platforms significantly more vulnerable or less valuable. In particular, large surface vessels, such as aircraft carriers and maritime prepositioning ships, could be at risk—at least until opponents evolve capabilities to locate and attack space-based platforms before they dispense their weapons. Space-based directed-energy weapons could have a similar effect for long flights of aircraft in clear weather.

When these changes could occur is not clear. As we have pointed out, U.S. military vision documents give space weapons an air of eventual inevitability, even though there is no compelling reason for the United States to acquire them at this time. Scientific advisors to the DoD have recommended development of some space-based weapons as a component of the forces needed to implement the Chairman of the Joint Chiefs of Staff's vision of the U.S. military for 2010 and beyond. Official plans estimate their acquisition in the next 10 to 20 years (Estes, 1998), which would require a decision to develop them soon. The United States has a technology program for space-based laser weapons that is approaching demonstration of the ability to destroy missiles from space.

As this report suggests, before deciding to acquire or forgo space weapons for terrestrial conflict, the United States should fully discuss what they can do, what they will cost, and the likely consequences of acquiring them. The discussion should recognize that, whether the United States decides to acquire them or not, there is a reasonable chance that other countries may acquire them. The countries with the greatest incentive to acquire them are likely to do so covertly. The United States needs to anticipate which countries might acquire space weapons, how it could discern the acquisition, and how it could respond effectively.

SPACE-BASED DIRECTED-ENERGY WEAPONS

To illustrate the range of issues in sizing and basing a space-based laser, we will focus on one stressing mission, ballistic missile defense, and explore it quantitatively as a function of the missile targets and trajectories and of weapon characteristics, sizing and orbital basing. The allure of space-based lasers against these time-urgent targets is the possibility of extending the engagement down into the atmosphere and of initiating the engagement sooner, without having to first characterize the target's probable future trajectory in order to select weapons that can reach it in time.

SAMPLE PROBLEMS: BOOST-PHASE MISSILE DEFENSE

To quantify the different degrees of urgency in boost-phase missile defense, we will examine three different, representative target cases: short, medium, and intercontinental range. The specific trajectory parameters for these cases are summarized in Table A.1. The intercontinental range burnout times are typical for solid-propellant missiles. Older, liquid-propellant missiles typically have another couple of minutes of burn time. The time to reach 15 km altitude is highlighted to indicate the earliest time that a hydrogen-fluoride laser could engage. Lasers at wavelengths that penetrate deeper into the atmosphere can recover some portion of the previous 45 to 60 seconds—how much depends on when the surveillance system has the opportunity to see the launch unobscured by clouds. Given a total boost time of about 1.5 to 3 minutes, recovering any significant portion of the lower altitude could mean a big difference in a weapon's kill capacity against a salvo of missiles.

Table A.1
Target Ballistic Missile Trajectory Parameters

	Range (km)	Flight Time (sec)	Time to 15 km Altitude (sec)	Burnout Time (sec)	Burnout Altitude (km)	Highest Altitude (km)
Short	875	500	50	85	53	225
Medium	3,375	1,050	61	110	64	650
Intercontinental	7,825	1,650	44	180	248	1,125

Figure A.1 shows the shape of the trajectories, from launch to impact. Figure A.2 highlights the boost-phase portion of the same trajectories. To evaluate the effectiveness of various constellations of space-based lasers, we will need to anchor those trajectories at specific launch and target points. For the sake of illustration and variety, implying nothing for future likelihood and no nostalgia for past concerns, we will consider the short-range trajectory from Iraq to Israel, the medium-range trajectory from Korea to Guam, and the intercontinental trajectory from Russia to Washington, D.C.; the ground traces appear in Figures A.3 through A.5.

BASE-CASE LASER

To begin our exploration of space-based lasers, we will start with a target damage threshold at 10,000 joules/cm² (at the high end of the 1 to 30 kilojoule range discussed earlier, about 10,000 times the level needed to burn exposed human skin) and will require the laser to

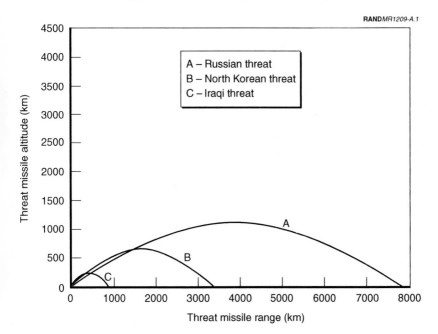

Figure A.1—Ballistic Missile Trajectories, Altitude Versus Range

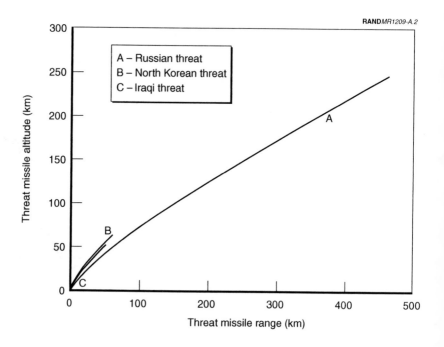

Figure A.2—Ballistic Missile Trajectories, Boost Phase

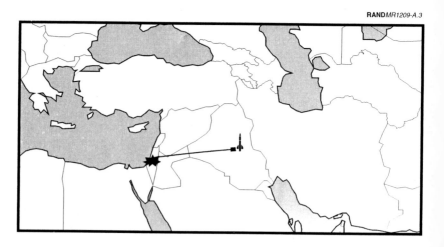

Figure A.3—Ballistic Missile Trajectory Ground Trace, Short Range

RAND*MR1209-A.4*

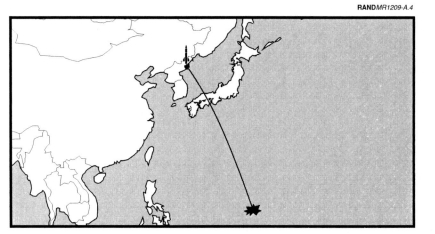

Figure A.4—Ballistic Missile Trajectory Ground Trace, Medium Range

RAND*MR1209-A.5*

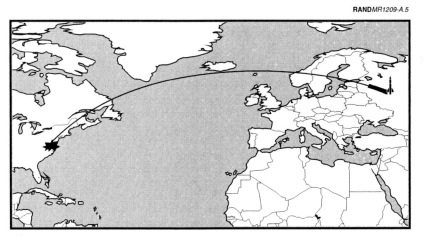

**Figure A.5—Ballistic Missile Trajectory Ground Trace,
Intercontinental Range**

provide that level of energy in a damage spot with a radius no smaller than 10 cm. The base case for our parametric calculations will be a hydrogen-fluoride laser, which operates at a wavelength of 2.7 μm (and is the space-based laser technology that has received the most funding and development). At that wavelength, the laser will receive credit for engagements beginning at altitudes above 15 km. The base-case laser will operate at a nominal power level of 5 megawatts. The base-case primary mirror will have a diameter of 10 m, with the secondary mirror and supporting structure obscuring 20 percent of that. We will assume the ability to retarget the laser to a new target within half a second[1] and the ability to hold its beam steady to a jitter level of 0.08 microradians, selected arbitrarily as consistent with ideal, diffraction-limited optical performance.

Given these parameters and the 49 seconds available from the time medium-range missile targets reach 15 km altitude until burnout, a single laser could expect to kill about three medium-range ballistic missiles out of a salvo from a range of about 1,700 km and a base altitude of about 550 km with an aspect angle of its line of sight to the target around 30 degrees off of broadside. In the process, it might consume on the order of 500 to 750 kg of laser fuel. The qualifications on that sample statement of capability are a reminder that the actual performance of space-based lasers results from a dynamic combination of factors that fluctuate over time and with the contributions of the entire constellation of lasers. The next section will explore the dynamics of that combination as a function of the constellation and individual laser parameters.

CONSTELLATIONS

Designing a constellation of satellites to provide service to the earth is a matter of selecting the number of satellites, their altitude, and their configuration in some number of orbit planes. Here, measures of performance and cost are the ordinary figures of merit. When the cost includes substantial ground equipment (such as communica-

---

[1]Although the angular distance the laser boresight must move through will decrease with distance and altitude and the effort needed to move it through that angle will increase with the size and mass of the laser and its optics, we will treat retargeting time as a constant here to illustrate the trends with a broad brush. More detailed engineering studies should include the additional effects.

tions terminals), the characteristics and costs of the ground equipment may dominate the design and shift expense into the satellites for a lower overall total cost. However, for these weapons, the ground equipment is limited to what is necessary to control the satellites and is not generally a large share of the total expense. Minimizing the overall cost will generally mean minimizing the cost of the portion of the system in space.

Minimizing the cost of the space segment of a weapon system is often misinterpreted as minimizing the number of satellites. Fewer satellites for a given earth coverage mean either that the orbits must be higher to allow a satellite to see more of the earth at once or that the satellites must be spaced farther apart in the planes of their orbits. Both approaches increase the range a laser weapon must reach, and the size and cost of the weapon increase with the square of the range. The second approach also requires a directed-energy weapon to propagate its energy through more atmosphere at shallower angles, which further increases the size and cost. Bearing that generalization in mind, let us examine a specific example.

Figure A.6 is a snapshot of the positions of a constellation of 24 space-based lasers. Each laser is at an orbital altitude of 1,248 km,

RAND*MR1209-A.6*

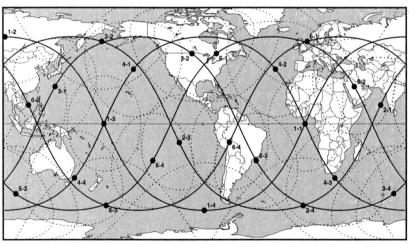

Figure A.6—Space-Based Laser Constellation Snapshot

and one orbit takes a little more than 110 minutes. The 24 satellites are divided into six groups of four. Each group occupies a plane or ring, with the six planes inclined 60 degrees to the equator and evenly spaced around the equator. The four satellites in each plane are evenly spaced around their orbital plane. The satellites in a plane are offset a sixth of an orbit from those in adjacent planes.

The solid lines that undulate over the map are the ground traces of the subsatellite points of an orbital plane at single moment. The labels indicate which satellite is on which path: Satellite m-n is in orbit position n in ring (plane) m. Following the ground trace from left to right shows which ones are ascending or descending on that path. The dotted lines depict the coverage of each satellite at the time shown. The coverage is limited to the 15-km altitude established for a hydrogen-fluoride laser. Taking one satellite as an example, number 1-3, there is a four-pointed star shaped area directly under it where it alone has coverage of targets. That star is bounded by convex lens-shaped areas where the satellite shares coverage with another, adjacent satellite. At the ends of two of those lens-shaped areas are areas where three satellites may engage targets. These shapes shift continuously with time. To visualize the dynamics of this, superimpose the motion of the satellites around their rings every 110 minutes on the motion of the surface of the earth under them every 24 hours. To translate this into constellation lethality, factor in the inverse-square effect of range and the projection[2] of each engaging weapon's line of sight onto the target.

The dynamic translation from geometry to lethality is difficult to visualize but straightforward to compute. Figure A.7 resulted from computing this for the base-case constellation of lasers against a salvo launch of medium-range ballistic missiles from Korea against Guam. The figure shows the number of missiles that the constellation could kill as a function of the time of launch, minute by minute, throughout the day. The graph resembles an amplitude modulation of a higher frequency wave by a lower frequency wave. The high-

---

[2]As a target's vulnerable surface is angled away from the line of sight of the laser, the laser's beam is projected over a larger area, diffusing its intensity. As the laser beam has to propagate to longer ranges, the area it projects grows with the square of the range, again diffusing its intensity correspondingly.

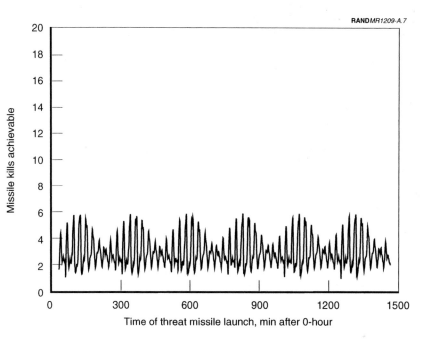

Figure A.7—Example Space-Based Laser Kill Capacity

frequency variation is tied to the time it takes satellites to orbit the earth. The time between the rapidly varying peaks (or, equivalently, valleys) corresponds precisely to one-fourth of the 110-minute orbital period, reflecting the spacing between the four satellites in a ring. Each peak in the short variation corresponds to the passage of a laser satellite over the launch point (or as nearly over it as the orbital plane allows at that time of day).[3]

The slower variation is tied to the earth's rotation under the constellation. The time between peaks of the slow variation corresponds to one-sixth of the 24-hour period of the earth's rotation. Drawing a horizontal latitude line across the map in Figure A.6 at the launch point to trace its path under the orbit planes through the day illus-

---

[3]The rapidly varying peaks would be even higher, because the beam spot size shrinks with decreasing range and increases intensity, except that we have limited the spot size to a minimum of 10 cm and have deliberately defocused the beam to keep the spot at the minimum when proximity would otherwise have made it smaller.

trates where the slow peaks and valleys occur. The valleys occur when the launch point is under areas farthest from the ground traces of the orbital planes. The peaks occur when the launch point passes closest to the intersections of the six ground traces of the orbital planes.

The shape of this pattern points out an important aspect of laser performance claims. The shape and timing of this pattern are predictable and readily available to any opponent sophisticated enough to have ballistic missiles. He will know when to launch a salvo to achieve the best penetration of the laser defense. He may not be confident of the relative hardness of his missiles against the power of the lasers (and so of the minimum salvo size needed to have some penetrate), but he will know with certainty when his best opportunities are. And they will be regular and frequent. This is not something the owner of the space-based lasers can prevent.

Because of their size, the lasers would be extremely difficult to hide or to maneuver enough to be unpredictable. The opponent could easily field a space surveillance capability to keep track of them but, thanks to the Internet, would probably not need to have his own tracking capability. Amateur astronomers are likely to publish the orbits electronically.[4] The opponent will certainly time his missile launches to coincide with the lowest points.

Claims of laser constellation lethality should be checked carefully for their assumptions about the timing of launch. A claim at the maximum kill rate assumes a willfully self-destructive opponent. A claim based on the average assumes a blissfully oblivious opponent. Only a claim based on the minimum is reasonable for this class of time-urgent targets. Any apparent excess of maximum over minimum kill rate capacity is surplus or wasted (at least for this target).

However, for slower targets or alternative missions in which the laser's owner can choose the time and geometry of engagement, this surplus target capacity could be put to use without compromising the constellation's capability against ballistic missile targets, which would presumably avoid launching at times of peak lethality. For example, a laser whose wavelength has been chosen to penetrate low enough into the atmosphere could be used against airplanes or

---

[4]The SeeSat-L Internet mailing list is an example; see Clifford and DePontieu (1994).

cruise missiles in flight or even against terrestrial targets, such as above-ground fuel tanks, missiles still on their launchers or transporters, fuel trucks, and other relatively thin-skinned or flammable targets. To the degree that such targets are vulnerable to the kind of surface-heating damage that a laser can inflict, engaging them should require amounts of laser fuel similar to those for a missile target.[5] Of course, any use of the excess kill rate capacity would still have to fit within the logistic limits of energy storage (electrical or chemical) and replenishment.

Certain approaches to weapon and constellation design could reduce the two sources of variation in kill rate capacity we observed in the base case. The approaches can be used separately or in combination. Reducing the large, rapid variation associated with the passage of a satellite over the target area requires reducing the relative range-to-target difference between the minimum and maximum engagement ranges. This can be done by adding lasers to reduce the spacing between them and increase the overlap of their coverage, which will reduce the range of angle away from the local vertical, where a single laser would have to carry the burden alone. Adding more lasers in additional orbital planes to reduce the spacing between rings would reduce or fill in the gaps that provide the slow variation.

Alternatively, having fewer lasers requires increasing their altitude to smooth out the variation in kill capacity. Of course, maintaining lethality at the longer ranges would require a corresponding increase in laser power (and/or aperture). Number, size, and orbit altitude determine the logistic cost of deploying and sustaining the constellation. Size and power, which determine fuel consumption in operation of the lasers, influence the logistic costs of operation. Figure A.8 shows the effect for the same target of raising the lasers from the base-case altitude of 1,248 km to 3,367 km (see Table A.2 for a summary of the parameters varied across the various laser case figures). To compensate for the increased range, we have increased the laser's

---

[5]The engagement could require less for nonlethal and indirect effects, such as illumination or stimulating fluorescence in aircraft canopy materials to degrade the pilot's view out of the cockpit. The laser could also presumably pick the times of engagement to take advantage of the shortest ranges to target.

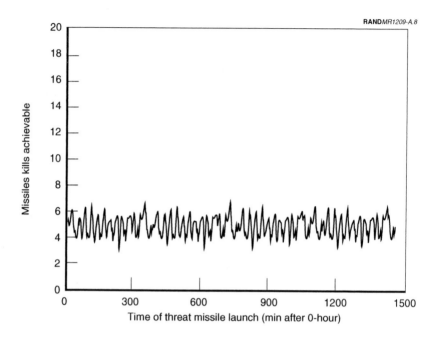

Figure A.8—Space-Based Laser Kill Capacity, Higher-Altitude Constellation

power to 35 megawatts, but we have cut the number of lasers on orbit in half to twelve. The rapid variations in kill capacity that we saw in Figure A.7 are broadened by the increase in orbital period to 159 minutes and smoothed out by the relatively flatter difference between minimum and maximum target ranges.

In the other direction, Figure A.9 shows the effect of reducing the altitude roughly by half, to 550 km; increasing the number of satellites by a factor of five; and decreasing the individual laser power by a factor of five from the base case. To the degree that the logistic cost for the entire constellation depends on the total weapon power on orbit, the cost for this much-larger constellation of smaller lasers should be similar to that of the base case. However, this constellation's performance against the ballistic missile threat is much better. Its profile is not as smooth as those of the base and the highest-altitude orbit (its orbital period, 96 minutes, is slightly less than that of the base case), but the magnitude of the swing between high and

Table A.2

Key to Laser Cases

Figure	Laser Type	Laser Wavelength (μm)	Minimum Altitude (km)	Laser Power (Mw)	Laser Aperture (m)	Laser Orbit Altitude (km)	Number of Lasers	Target Missile Range	Case Description
3.2	HF	2.7	15	5	10	1248	24	Medium	Base case
A.7	HF	2.7	15	35	10	3367	12	Medium	Higher altitude
A.8	HF	2.7	15	1	10	550	120	Medium	Lower altitude
A.9	HF	2.7	15	1	10	550	120	Short	Short-range targets
A.10	HF	2.7	15	1	10	550	120	Long	Long-range targets
A.11	COIL	1.3	5	1	10	550	120	Medium	Short wavelength
A.12	DF	3.8	5	1	10	550	120	Medium	Long wavelength
A.13	FEL	0.351	0	35	10	3367	2[a]	Medium	Relay mirrors

[a]Two ground lasers and 24 relay mirrors.

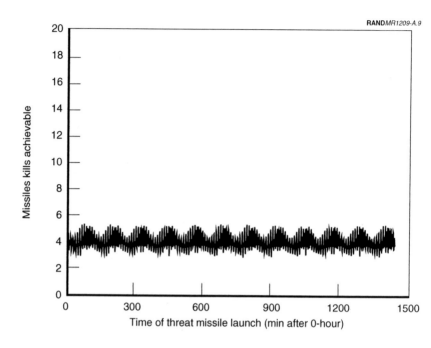

Figure A.9—Space-Based Laser Kill Capacity, Lower-Altitude Constellation

low is smaller than in the base case, and the minimum capacity is higher than in the base case. As an added benefit, this constellation is much more robust to failure or loss of an individual laser.

The difference between minimum and maximum kill capacity for the different orbital altitudes is primarily due to the way that the range to target varies with altitude as the laser engages targets at angles directly below it as opposed to those at the "horizon." Where the horizon falls depends on how closely the lasers are spaced and the altitude at which they can begin engaging targets. Table A.3 gives the range, angle, and relative (to the shortest range) power needed at the horizon for the 15-km minimum target altitude for the hydrogen-fluoride laser.[6]

---

[6]For a given orbital altitude, we could reduce the angle and range to the horizon by adding lasers to reduce the spacing between them as we did in the lower-altitude vari-

Table A.3

Hydrogen-Fluoride SBL Horizon Parameters

Orbit Altitude (km)	Angle to Horizon from Nadir (deg)	Range to Horizon (km)	Relative Power Needed at Horizon vs. Nadir
554	67	2680	24.7
1248	57	4158	11.8
3367	41	7355	4.8

MISSILE TARGET VARIATIONS

For these constellation trends, the driving factors are short missile flight times and the limited range of accessible target altitudes. Figures A.10 and A.11 help illustrate the urgency of the missile problem by comparing the variations in laser power and constellation against the data for shorter- and longer-range missiles from Table A.1. Figure A.9 shows the performance of a large, low-altitude, small-laser constellation against a short-range missile launched from Iraq to Israel. Against this more stressing, shorter-range missile, the constellation's minimum kill capacity is about 2. Figure A.10 shows the performance of the same constellation against the longer-burning, longer-range, intercontinental missile launched from Russia to Washington, D.C. Now, the constellation's minimum kill capacity is about 12.

WAVELENGTH

Laser wavelength is another variable. If the laser's power and the physical size of its optics are kept constant, changing the wavelength of the laser will change how well the optics can focus the energy on the target.[7] Shorter wavelengths will do better. The wavelength in

---

ation above. We could also increase the spacing between lasers and engage targets above the horizon at greater ranges, but the lasers' effectiveness falls off with the square of the increased range, and we would give up the time it takes the target to reach the higher engagement altitude.

[7]This presumes that the shape of the optical surfaces remains accurate to the corresponding tolerance of the new wavelength.

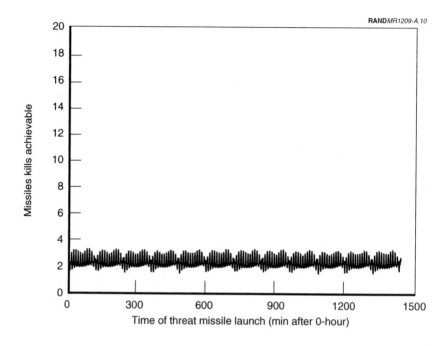

**Figure A.10—Space-Based Laser Kill Capacity, Lower-Altitude
Constellation, Short-Range Missile Target**

Figure A.9 was 2.7 µm; in Figure A.12, the wavelength has been
decreased to 1.3 µm, corresponding to replacing the hydrogen-
fluoride laser with an oxygen-iodine laser. The change in wavelength
should improve the kill rate by roughly a factor of four because of the
tighter focus at most ranges. This does not account for defocusing to
keep the energy at the minimum spot size at the shortest ranges with
the shorter wavelength.[8]

Another significant source of improvement with this change in
wavelength is that this wavelength propagates better through a window in the atmosphere's absorption profile, yielding the opportunity

---

[8]The shorter-wavelength laser could focus to about 80 percent of the minimum spot
size assumed for the 15-km target altitude directly below the laser.

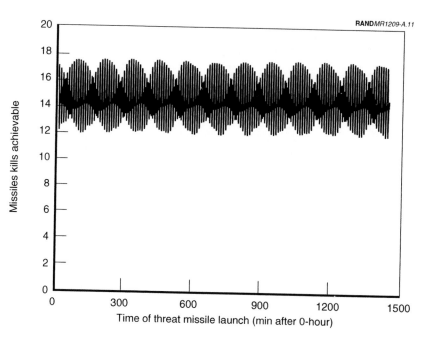

Figure A.11—Space-Based Laser Kill Capacity, Lower-Altitude
Constellation, Long-Range Missile Target

to engage targets at lower altitudes. Figure A.12 gives the constellation of lasers credit for being able to engage missile targets at altitudes as low as 5 km.

Figure A.13 examines the performance of the example constellation against a medium-range missile salvo but with a longer-wavelength laser to penetrate farther into the atmosphere than the hydrogen fluoride baseline. Instead of hydrogen fluoride, this laser is deuterium fluoride, with a wavelength of 3.8 µm. The figure gives credit for reach into the atmosphere to missile targets at a minimum altitude of 5 km. Increasing the wavelength should reduce the kill capacity by a factor of two because the focusing ability decreases for the same size mirror. However, the increased reach into the atmosphere has kept this constellation's performance on a par with the hydrogen-fluoride laser. This is not to say that deuterium is a good choice. Aside from

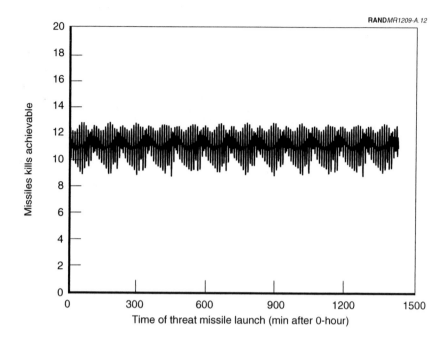

Figure A.12—Space-Based Laser Kill Capacity, Shorter Wavelength

its longer wavelength, it is a very rare isotope of hydrogen and likely to be expensive. Other things being equal, we would probably prefer the oxygen-iodine laser to either the hydrogen- or deuterium-fluoride lasers.[9]

RELAY MIRRORS

Once the choice of a suitable wavelength has moved the laser's effect on targets further into the atmosphere, the next conceptual step is to move the entire laser down to the earth's surface, keeping only the

---

[9]Among the other things that are not equal, oxygen-iodine lasers have not been in development as long as hydrogen-fluoride lasers. Also, a political, arms control, or other external imperative *not* to be able to engage targets deeper into the atmosphere from space could rule out the benefits of the shorter-wavelength laser.

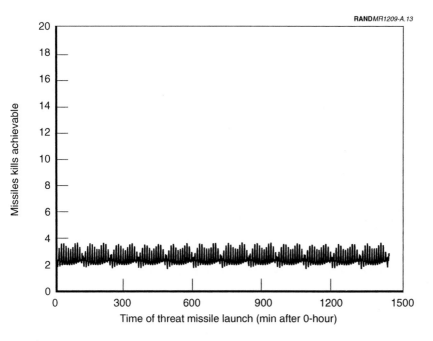

Figure A.13—Space-Based Laser Kill Capacity, Longer Wavelength

mirrors in space to redirect the energy to targets around the globe. This has the significant benefit of moving the logistic problem of replenishment to the ground, where transportation is less expensive. It has the additional benefit of largely eliminating the laser absentee problem and limiting absenteeism to the relay mirrors.

Some degree of redundancy in the ground-based lasers is, however, still necessary. Bad weather over the ground-based laser could cause it to be just as absent from the fight as a satellite-based laser whose orbit has carried it away from the target. There must be enough lasers located far enough away from each other to be confident that at least one site will have clear weather when a weapon is needed. This might be as few as two locations, say Hawaii and somewhere in the desert Southwest of the United States, depending on the climatology of the locations and the degree of assurance needed. But the absentee ratio here would still be a lot lower than those for the space-based components.

For the sake of propagation, the preferred locations for lasers will have dry climates (at least at the altitude of the laser) and high altitudes, such as mountaintops. A mountaintop would need infrastructure—roads, power, communications, and so forth. A handful of suitable mountains have already developed this kind of infrastructure to support astronomical observatories.[10] These locations also might be attractive for the ground-based laser component of relay system—assuming that the observatories have not run out of mountaintop real estate and that the laser's normal operation can be made compatible with the astronomical observations. The larger earthbound astronomical telescopes have begun sounding the atmosphere with laser guide stars to correct their own observations through adaptive optics. This might make a colocated laser weapon compatible, since the laser weapon also needs a laser guide star. Astronomers might even welcome the laser if its large optics could also be used to increase observing time when not needed for weapon operations, maintenance, or training. Also note that the common technical interests make such observatories a logical place to look for covert development and emplacement of such laser weapons.

There is, however, a price to be paid in space for moving the resupply logistics and the laser itself to the ground. Once again, the dominant factor is distance. In space, the laser weapon has the advantage of shorter distance to its targets when they are in its line of sight. The relayed path will be longer, unless the targets are relatively near the laser.[11] Over the longer path, the beam would ordinarily diverge and diffuse within the angle in which the originating mirror could concentrate the energy, the intensity of the beam at the target being divided by the square of the distance traveled. This could be done with a single large, flat mirror at each point along the way, angled to deflect the beam to its next destination and with the size of the mirror at each point increasing as the beam travels. It would be more practical, however, to use two large bifocal primary mirrors at each relay point connected to each other by a secondary optical path of smaller

---

[10]These include the observatories atop Arizona's Kitt Peak (AURA, 1999), New Mexico's Sacramento Peak (NOAO, 1999), California's Mt. Hamilton (UCO, 1999), and Hawaii's Mauna Kea and Haleakala volcanoes (Wainscoat, 1997; Maberry, 1998).

[11]In that unlikely case, something other than a space-based weapon would be more appropriate for local defense.

mirrors, much as the space-based laser would be connected to its large primary mirror. One of the bifocal mirrors would capture the incoming beam and the other would refocus it on its way. Compared with the space-based laser constellations in the previous section, moving the lasers to the ground effectively doubles the number of large mirrors in space.[12] All the mirrors require the same kind of precise, stable pointing as the space-based laser's mirrors but are at least not physically connected with the laser's mechanical disturbances. Because the beam inevitably spills some beyond the edges of the capturing mirror(s) in the relay, some additional power is lost at each relay. The saving grace of this arrangement is that it should be easier to make up the losses with a higher-power laser because the cost of emplacing and supporting a smaller number of lasers on the ground is lower.

The effects of orbital basing on the mirrors for the relay architectures parallel those for the space-based laser architectures in the previous section. To illustrate this, Figure A.14 plots kill capacity for the medium-range missile threat throughout the day for a constellation of 24 10-m diameter bifocal relay mirrors orbiting at an altitude of 3,367 km. Two 35 megawatt lasers, hypothetically in Albuquerque, New Mexico, and operating at the free-electron laser wavelength of 0.351 μm, complete the system.[13] The mirror altitude is similar to that in Figure A.7. The laser power is about seven times greater, which balances reasonably with the longer path lengths. Also, the number of mirrors and the laser wavelength are different. The higher power and shorter wavelength are responsible for the apparent improvement over Figure A.7.[14]

---

[12]There have been proposals to reduce the total number of mirrors in a relay architecture by giving them a mixture of high- and low-altitude orbits. The idea was to use a small number of very large "relay" mirrors at high altitudes and a larger number of smaller "fighting" mirrors at lower altitudes. Generally, depending on the difficulty and cost of the optics, these architectures do not perform as well as or cost less than architectures of self-relaying fighting mirrors at lower altitudes.

[13]Note that this laser would require correspondingly more-stringent pointing than the longer-wavelength lasers used in the space-based examples.

[14]We also gave the ground-based laser credit for lower jitter, which contributes some to the improvement.

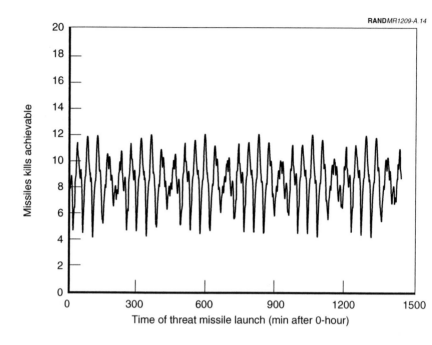

Figure A.14—Space-Based Laser Kill Capacity, Relay Mirror Constellation

KINETIC-ENERGY SPACE WEAPONS

Chapter Three introduced kinetic-energy weapons for striking earth from space by referring to the natural phenomenon of meteoroids. Here, we present an idealized discussion of the physics of meteoroids to develop a quantitative understanding of the physics of kinetic-energy weapon reentry. The appendix then describes the physics of hypervelocity impact and translates this into elements of weapon design and goes on to explore the trade-offs in responsiveness, logistic effort, lethality, and accuracy that constrain the selection of particular orbital basing alternatives. The appendix concludes by extending the exploration to the delivery of conventional munitions from space, where some constraints are relaxed.

IDEALIZED METEOROIDS

Figures B.1 and B.2 plot velocity and acceleration against height for some idealized spherical iron meteoroids (325 and 60 metric tons) and stone (325, 60, 30, and 5 metric tons) entering earth's atmosphere at 20 km/sec and an angle of 60 degrees below horizontal. A comparison of the traces of like material and traces of like mass reveals two effects: For a given material, the lower-mass objects decelerate at higher altitudes. For a given mass, the denser iron objects retain more of their initial velocity to impact. The determining factor for the different trajectories is the tug-of-war between the mass (or inertia) of the object retaining velocity and the force of atmospheric drag. That tug-of-war is captured quantitatively by the ballistic coefficient (β): the ratio of the object's mass to its drag coefficient times

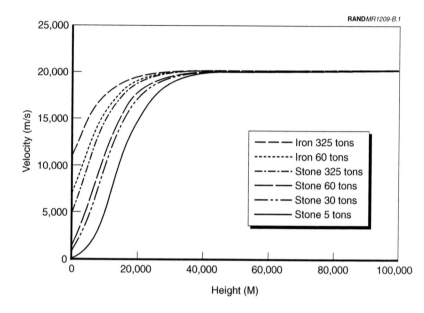

Figure B.1—Velocity, Idealized Spherical Meteoroids
(entry at 20 km/s and 60°)

the projected area of its cross section.[1] A projectile with a higher β
retains more of its velocity while transiting the atmosphere. Because
the kinetic energy we would like these weapons to retain after their
transit of the atmosphere is half the product of the weapon's mass
and its velocity squared, a weapon with a higher β will be more efficient than one with a lower β—if it can survive the heat and forces of
reentry intact.

The general shape and the magnitude of deceleration are the same
for all these different meteoroids. The altitude of greatest deceleration is a function of the β. The higher-mass, smaller-area (higher β)
iron meteoroids begin decelerating lower in the atmosphere and
retain more velocity to the surface. The peak magnitude of decelera-

_____
[1]An alternative definition uses weight instead of mass.

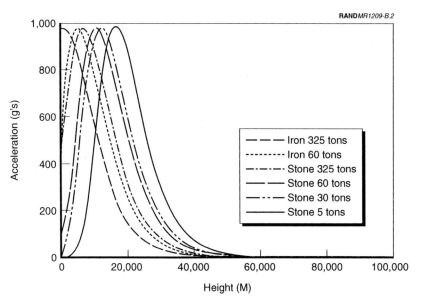

**Figure B.2—Acceleration, Idealized Spherical Meteoroids
(entry at 20 km/s and 60°)**

tion is a function of the initial reentry velocity.[2] Objects with the
same β encountering the atmosphere at lower velocities undergo less
stressful decelerations. Figure B.3 shows that the acceleration profiles of the 325-ton iron meteoroid of Figure B.2 become gentler as
initial velocities decrease from 20 to 15 and 10 km/s. The next section will translate these idealized meteoroids into artificial meteoroids to explore the issues in designing kinetic-energy weapons
from space.

---

[2]Among the ways that this portrayal idealizes meteoroids is in the assumption of
structural integrity under loads of this magnitude. Real stony meteoroids in this size
range undergoing this kind of deceleration and heating would break apart into smaller
fragments with smaller βs. Many are apparently rubble piles resulting from collisions
in space over their lifetimes, only loosely held together by their own gravity (Asphaug,
2000). However, these idealized trajectories do include the effect of losing material to
ablation as the intense heat of reentry vaporizes material on the surface of the object.

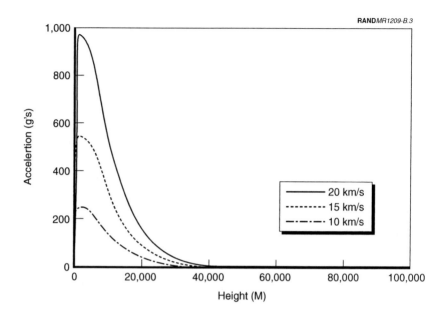

Figure B.3—Acceleration, Idealized 325-Ton Iron
Spherical Meteoroid (entry at 60°)

ARTIFICIAL METEOROIDS

Artificial meteoroids for use as kinetic-energy weapons would
preferably consist of materials that would increase the destructive
energy at impact for a given mass of weapon material, since the expense and even the feasibility of moving the weapon will depend on
its mass. In the natural analog, iron appears to be more efficient
than stone. Something like tungsten might be a good choice for our
imaginary artificial meteoroids. Tungsten is one of the densest materials available (19.25 metric tons/m³; iron is 7.87). It has a higher
heat capacity and melting point than most materials, which would
help it to survive the intense heat of entry. It is readily available and
relatively inexpensive.[3] Figure B.4 shows the kinetic energy of 325-

---

[3]The U.S. produces about 3,000 to 5,000 metric tons of tungsten metal powder annually (USGS, 1998), at a price of about $50 per pound (Woolman, 1996). Ore that is a
minimum of 65 percent tungsten trioxide costs about $40 to $50 per metric ton (USGS,
1998). Depleted uranium is marginally more dense, somewhat less expensive, and

ton spherical "meteoroids" of stone, iron, and tungsten entering earth's atmosphere at 20 km/s.[4] Tungsten is visibly more efficient at delivering destructive energy to earth's surface after reentry through the atmosphere.

Given an efficient material for artificial meteoroids, how do the weapon effects scale as velocity decreases from meteoroid velocities to those of satellites and ICBMs and as mass decreases enough to make lifting it within earth's gravity well reasonable with known propulsion technology? Figures B.5 and B.6 and Table B.1 show the effect of reducing the initial velocity to a representative orbital reentry velocity of 11 km/s and of incrementally reducing the size of the tungsten spheres. As sphere radius decreases from 1 m to 50 cm, im-

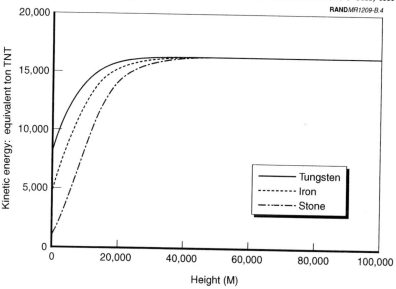

Figure B.4—Kinetic Energy, Idealized Spherical 325-Ton Meteoroids (entry at 20 km/s and 60°)

more readily pyrophoric (spontaneously combustible) than tungsten but has been subjected to substantial public scrutiny for health hazards since the Persian Gulf War (Fahey, 1998).

[4]Note that this reflects only the kinetic energy. For some materials, there may also be destructive energy due to chemical effects on impact.

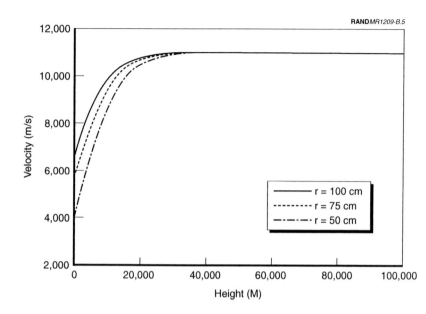

Figure B.5—Velocity, Tungsten Sphere (entry at 11 km/s)

pact velocity and kinetic energy decrease rapidly. The 1-m sphere retains about 34 percent of its kinetic energy (and about 99 percent of its mass and β) to impact; the 75-cm sphere, about 24 percent (a little more than 98 percent of its mass and β); and the 50-cm sphere, only 11 percent (95 percent of its β and 96 percent of its mass) to impact.

Looking at weapon efficiency in another way, the smallest sphere delivers the equivalent of about 1.7 tons of TNT per ton of weapon; the medium, 3.6; and the large 5.2. Avoiding this reduction in efficiency as size decreases would be helpful for scaling down from crater-making meteoroids to useful weapons. Aside from the reduction in efficiency with reduced weapon size, the impact velocities, while still high enough to hurt, are beginning to fall below the levels at which hypervelocity effects occur.[5] Retaining the efficiency of a

---

[5]Hypervelocity damage effects require impact velocities higher than the speed of sound in the target material, e.g., for stone about 4 km/s, for steel about 6 km/s.

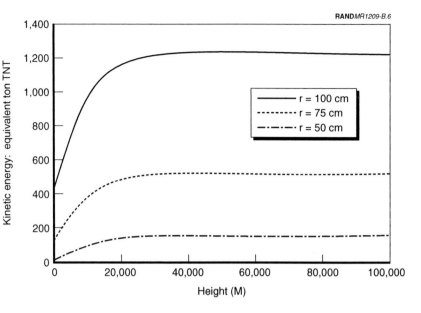

RAND*MR1209-B.6*

**Figure B.6—Kinetic Energy, Tungsten Sphere
(entry at 11 km/s)**

Table B.1

Tungsten Sphere Entries from 11 km/s at 60°

Initial Radius (cm)	Initial Mass (metric tons)	Initial Ballistic Coefficient (Pascals)	Impact Velocity (km/s)	Impact Kinetic Energy (tons TNT)
50	10	62,880	3.7	17
75	34	94,320	5.4	124
100	80	125,800	6.5	422

kinetic-energy weapon as weapon mass decreases means finding a way to keep the β high by reducing drag.

SCALING TO USEFUL WEAPONS

In contrast to the artificial meteoroids of the last section, a tactically useful weapon should achieve effects measurable in fractions of equivalent tons of TNT, with mass measured in kilograms, not tons. The weapon should be small enough to allow delivery to all the desired targets at a reasonable logistic cost—preferably one lower than for other means of destroying the same targets. This requires maintaining a high β while reducing the weapon's mass, by reducing the contribution of drag.

Conceptually, this is straightforward. Instead of reducing all the dimensions of the sphere uniformly, which will reduce the β proportionately, reduce the projected frontal area, resulting in something like an elongated rod. Reasonable shapes, such as those developed for ICBM reentry vehicles, can increase the β by about 100 times over a sphere of equivalent mass. The classic ICBM reentry vehicle (see Figure B.7) is an elongated, sphere-capped cone. The slight flare at the base provides better directional aerodynamic stability than a rod, and blunting the cone with the cap reduces heating. Table B.2 lists representative ICBM reentry vehicle characteristics.

While this representative reentry vehicle has a reasonable size for existing rockets to launch, the tungsten sphere trajectories suggest that the β should be higher for a kinetic-energy weapon. A slightly more slender, 1-m-long tungsten reentry vehicle would produce a similar mass and a β three to five times greater than the representative reentry vehicle. This would produce trajectories with impact velocities of tungsten spheres weighing tens of tons. However, even at similar impact velocities, the effects of these slender, rodlike weapons will be qualitatively different from those of the crater-making spheres, which will restrict the targets they can be used against.

Although a higher β increases the kinetic energy available on impact, there are limits in practice. Atmospheric density increases exponentially with decreasing altitude, and the heat loading increases in proportion. The increasing velocity itself further increases the heat loading, proportional to the cube of the velocity. Getting rid of the heat is a significant engineering challenge. Some of it is radiated away. Some is carried off in the flow field around the body. Some is absorbed in the material of the vehicle. However, with higher-β, lower-mass bodies, some of the heat must be eliminated by sacrificing some of the mass through sweating (transpiration) or melting away from the external surface (ablation). For this purpose, tungsten

RAND*MR1209-B.7*

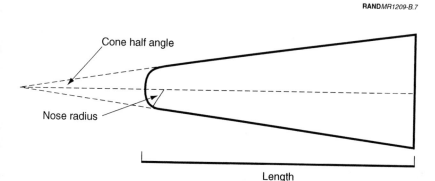

Figure B.7—Cross Section of Classic Reentry Vehicle

Table B.2

Representative Reentry Vehicle Characteristics

Nose radius (cm)	1.98
Base radius (cm)	22
Length (cm)	152
Mass (kg)	92
Drag coefficient	0.1
Ballistic coefficient (β)	60,000

SOURCE: Regan (1984), p. 333.

material is attractive not only for its density but for its attractively high melting and vaporization temperatures. The challenge is to maintain a predictably uniform shape and aerodynamic lift characteristics despite the ablation. Uneven ablation creates asymmetries that cause substantial, unpredictable lift, causing a miss. Figure B.8 shows the effects of ablation on a hand-sized iron meteoroid. The pitting visible in the photograph is uniformly present on all sides of the object. Although the initial shape and reentry conditions are unknown, it is clear that the pitting altered the aerodynamic characteristics significantly.

Thermal design is the most challenging aspect of this weapon class, and extrapolating beyond the ICBM reference point should be done cautiously. However, more-specific discussions of the engineering compromises would be classified and will not be pursued here.

RAND*MR1209-B.8*

SOURCE: Calvin Shipbaugh.

NOTE: The Sikhote-Alin iron meteorite fell in 1947 in the USSR between the Sea of Japan and China. The total energy released was equal to that from a low-yield weapon. The scale is inches.

Figure B.8—Fragment of Sikhote-Alin Iron Meteoroid with Ablative Pitting

That said, let us consider representative sizing of a hypothetical tungsten reentry body for a kinetic-energy weapon. The tungsten sphere trajectories gave us a target β. Making the spheres more slender and rodlike adds a new, design dimension—length—with critical effects on weapon performance.

Hypervelocity impacts have four distinct phases.[6] The first phase, the transient shock regime, begins at the moment of impact, when the leading edge of the projectile is brought to rest relative to the surface of the target. This generates very high pressures and temperatures and usually a brief impact flash. The second phase, the

---

[6]The description here follows Hermann and Wilbeck (1987, p. 308–309), which describes impacts into homogeneous, relatively ductile materials. Composite and more brittle materials propagate the shock differently after the steady-state regime; for example, concrete shatters and spalls.

steady-state regime, lasts while the projectile is eroded away as it continues to penetrate into the target material. The duration of this phase depends on the length of the projectile. The third phase, the cavitation regime, begins when the projectile is completely eroded away and the crater continues to expand under its own inertia. The fourth phase, the recovery regime, may reduce the size of the crater slightly as the target material rebounds.

If the projectile has a similar length and diameter, like our tungsten spheres, cavitation dominates the effects. The size of the crater resulting from a short, squat projectile depends on the projectile's total kinetic energy and the target's hardness. If the angle of impact produces a component of the velocity vector into the target that is greater than the speed of sound in the target material, the crater will be hemispherical. For more glancing impacts, the crater will elongate, becoming more elliptical. Either way, the damage proceeds downward and outward from the point of impact. In contrast, the damage for an ordinary explosive detonated at the same point would proceed outward in all directions.

If the projectile is long and rodlike, on the other hand, the steady-state phase dominates the effects. The crater is more cylindrical and its depth is proportional to the square root of the ratio of projectile density over target density. If the kinetic-energy weapon must penetrate shielding, e.g., a ship's hull or a bunker, the depth to be penetrated determines the minimum projectile length, depending on the density of the shielding material. For example, a 1-m-long tungsten hypervelocity penetrator should be able to penetrate about 1.5 m of steel, almost 3 m of clay or stone, and 1 m of uranium. What penetrates through that depth (or less) of target will be a very hot mixture of target and penetrator material and any remaining penetrator length. The damage is done almost entirely in the direction of the impact, as with a shaped charge explosive, except for damage caused by secondary fires or explosions ignited by the impact.[7]

---

[7]While room-temperature tungsten is a solid and not pyrophoric, hot tungsten vapor, liquid droplets, and small solid particles will combust. The portion of a penetrator that reaches atmosphere inside the target (say, in a bunker or inside a ship) in combustible form will act like an explosive charge.

ORBITAL BASING

Distance, time, gravity, and inertia impose some limits on a weapon that must deliver a mass to a target. Passage through the atmosphere also imposes some hard constraints on kinetic-energy weapons. To retain sufficient destructive energy after transiting the atmosphere, the weapon must begin reentry with a velocity that depends on the β of the reentry vehicle. Beginning reentry with a higher velocity requires either a higher orbit or additional propulsion and logistic costs.

A higher orbit has a number of desirable attributes. It can increase the weapon's footprint—the portion of earth's surface it can reach from a single starting point in orbit. A higher orbit can also make it more difficult to detect the initiation of an attack by reducing the amount of propulsion (and therefore the visibility of its signature) needed for deorbit and by increasing both the volume of space that must be watched and the distance between the defense's sensors and the weapon. But higher orbits increase the transit delay, the time between launch and target impact. The logistic cost per weapon to achieve orbit is also higher, although the lower cost to deorbit and the increased reach offset this somewhat.

Aside from providing a minimum reentry velocity, the orbital basing mode will have to provide a minimum angle of reentry off the vertical. Relative to a steeper reentry, a shallow angle forces travel through more of the atmosphere, thus slowing the weapon and giving defenses more time to react. A shallow reentry angle also magnifies any guidance errors. Ideally, to minimize miss distances, the trajectory through the atmosphere should be as straight and near vertical as possible. In practice, the trajectory should probably be within 30 degrees of vertical or at least 60 degrees below the horizontal.

Subject to the peculiar constraints of kinetic-energy weapons, the selection of a particular orbital basing approach is a compromise between interrelated factors, which the subsections below illustrate using both circular and elliptic orbits:

- response time

- logistic expense

- lethality
- target coverage or access.

Circular Orbits

One of the prime reasons for going to space, whether for weapons or any other purpose, is to achieve a global perspective. If the perspective and the interests are local, a terrestrial or atmospheric solution would often be more economical. And if there is enough time for such local solutions to get to the area of interest, a space solution may not be as economical as a terrestrial solution.

With the notable exception of a geosynchronous orbit,[8] the combination of earth's rotation and the orbital movement of satellites means that any one satellite will periodically be out of reach of its service area. Under the circumstances, the penalty of providing continuous ground coverage is additional satellites. If, however, periodic coverage is acceptable, fewer additional satellites may be necessary. Furthermore, space can be an economical way to achieve coverage that is more global, because the additional satellites would be covering multiple areas of interest. Space may also be economical when local systems (terrestrial or atmospheric) cannot reach a global target in time (at least, without extensive prepositioning).

Because circular (or nearly circular) orbits do not favor any part of an orbit with a longer dwell or slower velocity, they are more suitable than elliptical orbits for global interests. The elliptical orbits considered below are more suitable for interests in either the northern or southern hemisphere.

Responsiveness. There are limits to how quickly it is reasonable to deliver mass from space to ground. Some responsiveness claims have been optimistic. One credited the weapons with the ability to strike any target in the world within 1 hour of launch or within 12

---

[8]There is one altitude at which the period of a satellite in a circular orbit matches the rotation of the earth. Here, the satellite will appear to remain in one place in the sky overhead if the orbit is over the earth's equator (i.e., the plane of the orbit has an angle of inclination with respect to the equator of zero). If the orbit is inclined with respect to the equator, the satellite will appear to trace out a figure eight above and below the equator.

minutes from orbit (AF/XPX 1998, p. 104). While 1 hour from launch is reasonable; 12 minutes from orbit has some costly strings attached.

Figure B.9 shows the time necessary to reach the outer fringes of the atmosphere from orbit using a minimum-energy path for circular orbit altitudes of 500 to 32,000 km. The flight time is a function of the range over the ground to the impact point (measured in the plane of the orbit from the point on earth directly under the satellite—the *subsatellite point*—when deorbit begins).[9] As one would expect, the necessary deorbit times decrease as the altitude of the orbit de-

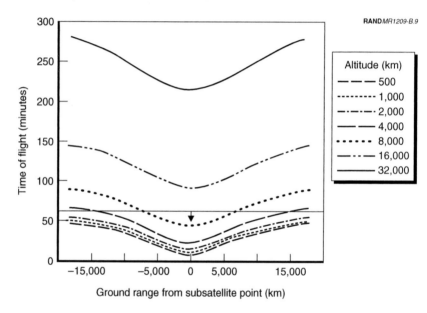

Figure B.9—Time to Reentry from Circular Orbit

---

[9]Note that the ground ranges in this appendix do not include the effect of earth's rotation, which would shift the footprint of a given trajectory, depending on the angle of inclination of the orbital plane relative to the equator. While this information is not necessary for determining how many positions are necessary for a degree of coverage, it would, of course, be necessary for selecting the particular orbital position from which to engage a specific target at a specific time.

creases. For a particular altitude, the times decrease according to how close the reentry point is to the deorbit point. At the lowest altitudes, a deorbit time of 12 minutes appears possible for ranges close to the deorbit point. But this is possible only within a fairly narrow range under the satellite—small enough to need around 40 to 150 satellites to provide global coverage. Worse, the constraints on reentry velocity and logistics of deorbit make it hard to find a workable compromise with the other constraints at this low altitude. The situation for higher altitudes improves, however, if circumstances permit a 1-hour delay.

Logistic Reach. One of the things that makes the shortest time for flight less desirable is the extra effort involved. The magnitude of the effort led an eminent group of scientists to advise President Dwight Eisenhower in 1958 against basing weapons in space:

> Much has been written about space as a future theater of war, raising such suggestions as satellite bombers, military bases on the moon, and so on. For the most part, even the more sober proposals do not hold up well on close examination or appear to be achievable at an early date. Granted that they will become technologically possible, most of these schemes, nevertheless, appear to be clumsy and ineffective ways of doing a job. Take one example, the satellite as a bomb carrier. A satellite cannot simply drop a bomb. An object released from a satellite doesn't fall. So there is no special advantage in being over the target. Indeed the only way to "drop" a bomb directly down from a satellite is to carry out aboard the satellite a rocket launching of the magnitude required for an intercontinental missile. A better scheme is to give the weapon to be launched from the satellite a small push, after which it will spiral in gradually. But that means launching it from a moving platform halfway around the world, with every disadvantage compared to a missile base on the ground. In short, the earth would appear to be, after all, the best weapons carrier. (Killian, 1977, p. 297.)

To understand the trade-off between time of flight and effort, we must calibrate the transition from "intercontinental missile" to "small push." The measure of that effort is the change in velocity (Δv) required to accelerate the weapon enough to achieve the desired deorbit path. Figure B.10 shows the Δv needed for the same minimum-energy trajectories as for the times of flight in Figure B.9. At

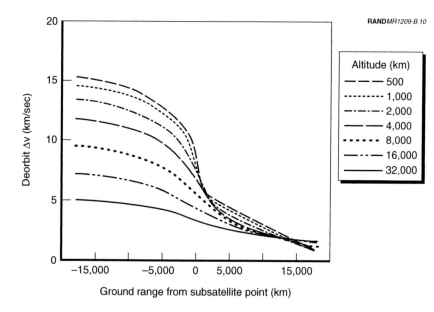

Figure B.10—Deorbit Δv from Circular Orbit

the lowest orbits, the magnitude for a "drop" from directly overhead is 7 to 8 km/sec—about the same as for an ICBM. As might be expected, the magnitude gets quickly worse when shooting at targets behind the deorbit point. However, things improve quickly as the targets move out ahead and as the altitude of the launching orbit increases. The small push, though, is still big enough to accelerate the weapon through a few km per second, enough to deliver a ground-based ballistic missile several hundred kilometers. The trends in this figure suggest that increasing the orbit altitude makes delivering the weapon significantly easier. However, the small push for deorbit is only part of the logistic effort needed to deliver the weapon to target.[10]

---

[10]The Δv needed is a convenient way to quantify the size of the push needed. Translating this effort into the mass required depends on the kind of propulsion system used. Later in this appendix, we will translate Δv into approximate mass of propellant needed for the total effort to deploy and deliver a given mass of these weapons. The cost for a given mass depends on the kind of propulsion, the number of vehicles, the degree of component reuse, etc.

A more-complete logistics picture has to include the total effort for inserting the weapon into orbit, circularizing that orbit, and deorbiting onto a target. Figure B.11 shows the total Δv required for the circular orbital basing and weapon trajectory alternatives used in Figures B.9 and B.10. Including the effort required to deploy the weapon to the higher altitude orbits, the total transportation cost for a weapon is uniformly higher for higher than for lower altitudes. However, the cost is not as sensitive over the range of reach for the higher as for lower altitudes. This contributes to a general trend toward greater reach from higher altitudes. The increased reach means that fewer weapons are needed to provide access to an equivalent area, which offsets the higher transportation cost per weapon at higher altitudes somewhat.

The area enclosed in the box in Figure B.11 indicates the logistic effort for delivering these kinds of weapons using suborbital, ballistic trajectories starting on earth's surface. The details will be explored later, but Eisenhower's advisors were right in one respect: Within the

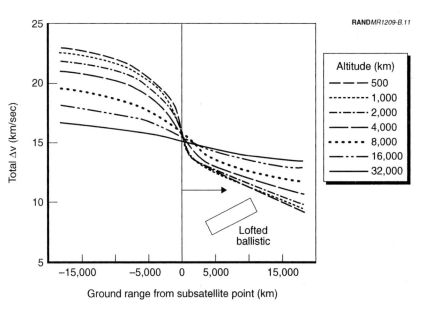

Figure B.11—Total Δv for Inserting, Circularizing, and Deorbiting
a Weapon from Circular Orbit

ranges that can be reached by ballistic trajectories, earth is indeed a better weapon carrier if *better* is measured only by the logistic difficulty of delivering a weapon.

Another trade-off between logistics and responsiveness is speed of deorbit. What about the possibility of expending some effort to deorbit faster than the minimum energy trajectory deorbit from base orbit allows? Figure B.12 shows (for the higher-altitude base orbits) the deorbit effort required as the time of flight to reentry decreases, as a fraction of the time for a minimum-energy deorbit trajectory. The data are for representative trajectories reaching about 3,000 km forward from the subsatellite point of the deorbit burn. Surprisingly, the first 40 to 50 percent of reduction in flight time comes at very little additional effort. This is not a peculiarity of the representative range selected. Figure B.13 shows the same trend over a broad range of reach for the 32,000-km-altitude base orbit. For higher-altitude orbits, it should be possible to discount the minimum energy responsiveness by 40 to 50 percent without significant logistic penalty. However, there is a limit to how low the discount is applicable.

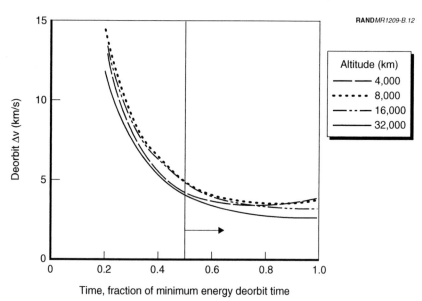

Figure B.12—Δv for Faster Deorbit at 3,340-km Ground Range

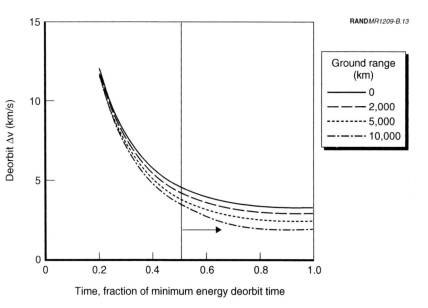

Figure B.13—Δv for Faster Deorbit from 32,000 km

The earlier discussion of weapon characteristics noted an accuracy constraint on the angle of the reentry flight path, nominally at no more than about 30 degrees off vertical or, equivalently, no less than 60 degrees below the horizontal. Speeding up the deorbit with a more-direct path necessarily flattens the trajectory. At lower altitudes, this could make the reentry flight path angle too shallow at longer ground ranges. Figure B.14 shows this effect for the altitudes and ground range shown in Figure B.12. At that range, decreasing the flight time by roughly half for altitudes above 16,000 km costs little additional effort. At 8,000 km, the time can only be decreased by about 30 percent before it begins to violate the shallow reentry constraint at this range. This constraint will come up again in the next subsection.

Lethality Constraints. Here, *lethality* means the ability to deliver the kinetic-energy weapon to a target with enough velocity to achieve the desired destructive effect. The weapon's orbital altitude affects the lethality by establishing the initial reentry velocity and flight-path

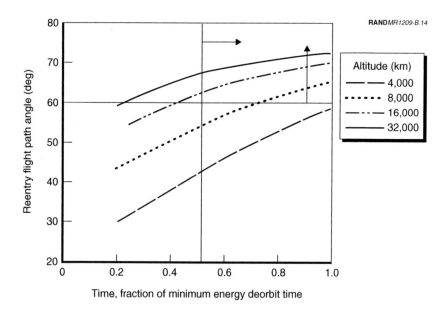

Figure B.14—Reentry Angle for Faster Deorbit at 3,340-km Ground Range

angle, which the weapon's physical characteristics translate into terminal velocity. Too shallow a flight path angle degrades accuracy and increases the extent of atmosphere the weapon has to transit. Figure B.15 shows the flight-path angle at reentry for the same variety of altitudes and ground ranges used in previous figures. At all altitudes, there is a limit to how far the target can be from the subsatellite point without making the reentry trajectory too shallow. The limiting effect is particularly severe at the lowest altitude but improves fairly quickly as altitude increases.

Unfortunately, while the reentry angle will be steep at the lowest altitudes (close to the subsatellite point), the reentry velocity will be its lowest. Figure B.16 shows the minimum-energy trajectory velocity at the beginning of reentry. At the lowest altitudes, even before the atmosphere bleeds off weapon speed, the velocity is too low for the desired effects against some targets. The impact velocity will depend on the specific β of the weapon; Figure B.17 shows predicted impact velocities for a representative weapon with the initial reentry condi-

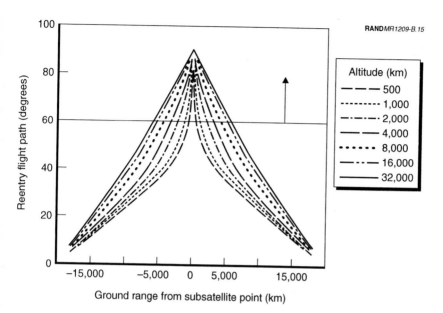

Figure B.15—Reentry Angle, Minimum Energy Deorbit from Circular Orbit

tions in Figures B.15 and B.16.[11] The effect of a shallow reentry angle is visible in the way the impact velocity profiles bend down at greater ground ranges (compare the profiles in Figure B.16). Close to the deorbit burn subsatellite point, where the low altitude, short time-of-flight cases are driven by reentry angle, the impact velocities are 2 to 4 km/sec lower than desirable for some target classes. Adding propulsion to the weapon would raise the impact velocity. But this would not be a good compromise for two reasons. First, targets close to the subsatellite point are already on the steep part of the effort curve, even without making up the shortfall in impact velocity (see Figure B.11). Adding another "hump" of 2 to 4 km/sec onto that steep part of the curve would likely make individual weapon costs prohibitive. Second, the increased individual weapon logistic cost must be multiplied by the number of weapons and orbiting plat

---

[11]In this case, a 1-m long tungsten sphere-capped cone with a nose radius of 1 cm, a cone half-angle of 3 degrees, and a base radius of 6 cm.

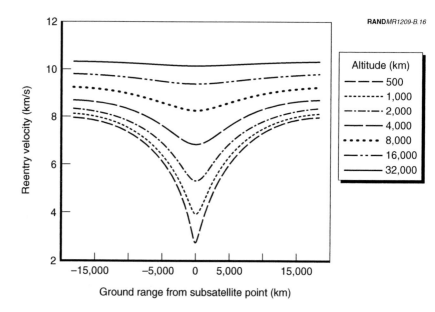

Figure B.16—Reentry Velocity Minimum Energy Deorbit
from Circu\lar Orbit

forms needed to compensate for the small footprint of any weapon. That multiplier is worse at lower altitudes. The next subsection will quantify this.

Target Coverage. Combining the constraints on individual weapon logistic effort (e.g., a maximum Δv of 15 km/s), accuracy (e.g., a reentry angle of ≥ 60 degrees), and impact velocity (e.g., about 6 km/sec), and examining trajectories both in the plane of the platform's orbit and cross-range from the plane can define a footprint reachable from a single orbiting weapon platform. If the goal is to provide on-call weapon response within some time constraint, there must be enough orbiting platforms to have one whose footprint will cover the target in time—including both the waiting time for the opportunity to shoot and the weapon time of flight from its altitude. A response time near 10 minutes from weapon release to target kill is too short for this class of weapon. However, a less-demanding scenario presents more reasonable compromises, starting with a

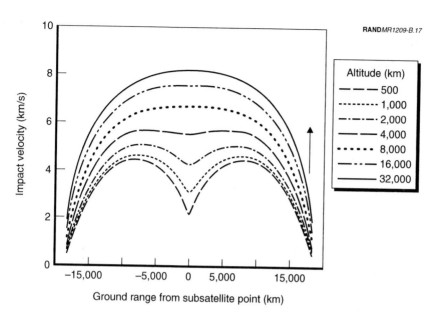

**Figure B.17—Impact Velocity Minimum Energy Deorbit
from Circular Orbit**

response time of about 1.5 to 2 hours and an altitude of about 4,000
to 32,000 km.

Table B.3 shows rough typical footprint constraints for 4,000 and
8,000 km altitude orbits. To illustrate all this more clearly, Figure
B.18 provides an orientation and Figures B.19 through B.22 are contour plots of the total delta velocity, time of flight to reentry, impact
velocity, and reentry angle for an altitude of 8,000 km altitude. Much
as a topographic map represents elevation by counturs, each map
here is a ground map (not shifted by earth's rotation) that presents
the value of the constrained parameter. The horizontal, in-range, direction of the map is in the plane of the satellite's orbit, and zero on
the scale is the subsatellite point where weapon deorbit begins. The
vertical, crossrange, direction is perpendicular to the orbital plane,
with zero directly under the path of the satellite that released the
weapon. Selecting a particular value for a trajectory parameter limits
the weapon's footprint to the area of corresponding contour on the

Table B.3

Typical Circular Orbit Footprints (km)

Constraint and Result	4,000 km Altitude		8,000 km Altitude	
	In-Plane	Cross-Range	In-Plane	Cross-Range
Total Δv <15 km/s	~1,000– 20,000	±5,000	~2,000– 20,000	±5,000
Reentry angle >60°	<3,000	±3,000	<4,000	±4,000
Impact velocity ~6 km/s	±10,000	±2,000	±10,000	±3,800
Resulting net footprint dimensions	~1,000– 3,000	±2,000	~2,000– 4,000	±3,800

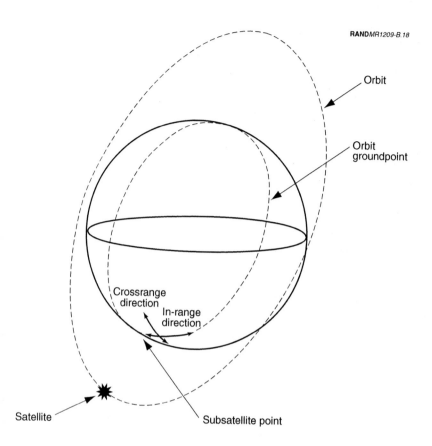

Figure B.18—Orbit Terminology

parameter's surface map. Constraining multiple parameters creates a footprint in which the different parameters' contours overlap. The values in Table B.3 roughly illustrate the process for these plots.

These footprints produce absentee ratios for global coverage in the mid-60s for an altitude of 4,000 km and in the mid-30s for 8,000 km, both for a response time of about 1 hour. Those are still pretty hefty. Raising the altitude to 32,000 km yields an absentee ratio of about 5. This would require us to accept a delay of about 2 to 3 hours (taking credit for a reduction in flight time from the minimum energy paths in Figure B.9 of about 60 percent, as in Figures B.12 and B.13). Limit-

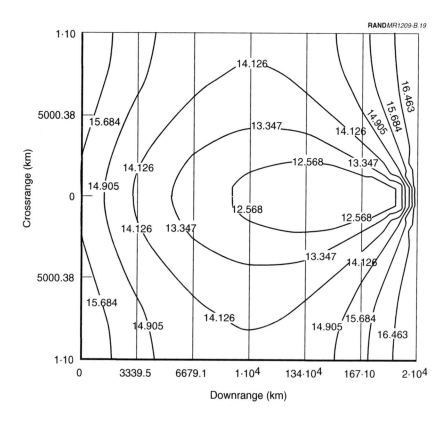

Figure B.19—Total Δv (km/s) for 8,000-km Circular Orbit

ing the target set to either the northern or southern hemisphere yields lower-cost alternatives in elliptical orbits.

Elliptical Orbits

Elliptical orbits are less expensive than corresponding circular orbits for two reasons: First, reducing the portion of the globe that can be reached with a weapon by roughly half reduces the number of orbital positions correspondingly. Second, the base orbit need not be circularized, so less logistical effort is needed for each weapon. Elliptical orbits may thus make sense, even for nearly global target needs.

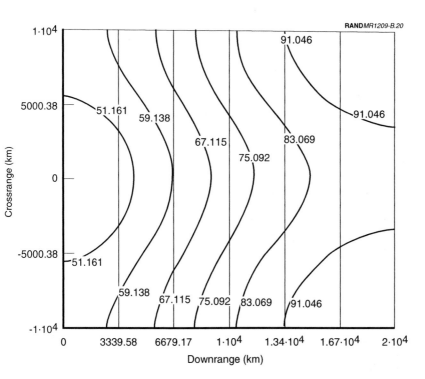

Figure B.20—Time of Flight to Reentry (min) from 8,000-km Circular Orbit, Minimum Energy Path

"Mirror-image" constellations, each covering either the northern or southern hemisphere, could provide more extensive coverage, although covering targets near the equator this way may be difficult.[12]

To provide a quantitative perspective on the differences between circular and elliptical orbit basing, Figures B.23 through B.30 graph a subset of the timeliness, logistic reach, lethality, and coverage constraints examined earlier for circular orbits. The representative

---

[12]The difficulty is that a satellite in an elliptical orbit spends most of the time in the high-altitude portions of its orbit, passing quickly over the low portion. To be usefully stable, the high-altitude portion will be over one or the other of the earth's poles. The footprint reach information shown for elliptical orbits in Figures B.23 through B.30 are for the highest points of the elliptical orbits.

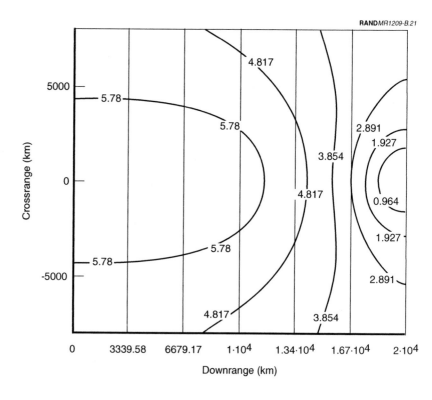

Figure B.21—Impact Velocity from 8,000-km Circular Orbit

elliptical orbits are summarized in Table B.4. The perigee height is selected to keep the satellite far enough above the atmosphere to prevent its orbit from decaying prematurely. The orbit lengths were selected as integer fractions and multiples of earth's rotation period to simplify visualization.[13]

Figure B.23 shows the time to reentry from apogee for the sample elliptical orbit. Generally, the minimum-energy time to deorbit is

---

[13]The integer relation with the earth's period of rotation is not essential, but it also helps to lock the orbit's ground trace to the earth, reducing some of the perturbing effects of irregularity in the earth's shape and, consequently, some of the satellite maneuver propellant needed to maintain desired orbit parameters.

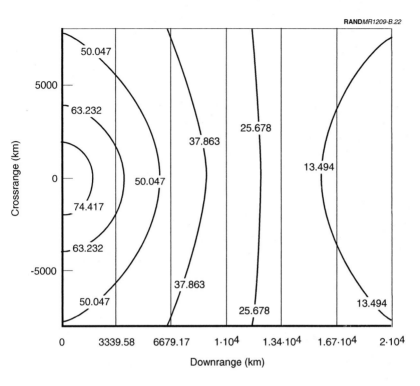

Figure B.22—Reentry Angle from 8,000-km Circular Orbit

about half the orbital period. For comparison with the reentry times similar to those used above for circular orbits, we will discuss only 3- to 12-hour elliptical orbits here.

Figure B.24 shows the corresponding total Δv needed for these orbits. The reasonable velocities here (10 to 12 km/sec) require substantially less effort per weapon than those for circular orbits (12 to 15 km/sec)—especially since the magnitude of rocket propulsion needed grows exponentially as the required Δv increases.

Figures B.25 and B.26 show the trends in accuracy (reentry angle) and lethality (impact velocity) for these orbits. In both respects, these orbits are more forgiving than circular orbits with similar re-

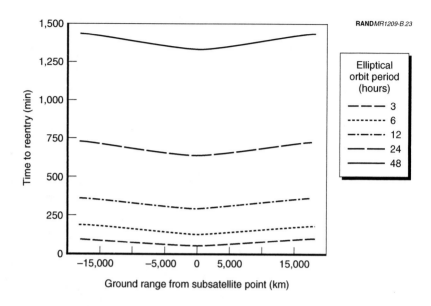

Figure B.23—Time to Reentry from 8,000-km Circular Orbit

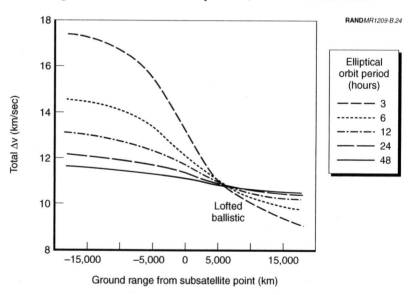

**Figure B.24—Total Insertion and Deorbit Δv for Minimum-Energy Deorbit
from Elliptical Orbit Apogee**

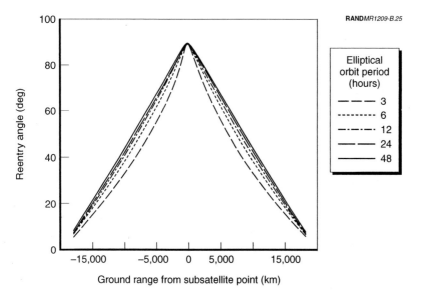

Figure B.25—Reentry Angle from 8,000 km for Minimum-Energy
Deorbit from Elliptical Orbit Apogee

sponsiveness. Combining the effects and comparing the 6-hour elliptical orbit with the 4,000- and 8,000-km circular orbits reveals that the elliptical orbit, for roughly comparable responsiveness, has better logistic reach, comparable accuracy, and better lethality within its hemispheric coverage.

Figures B.27 through B.30 are contour plots for the 6-hour elliptical orbit showing the in-range and crossrange footprints from apogee for total Δv, impact velocity, time of flight, and reentry angle. These footprints would result in an absentee ratio of 4 to 8 for hemispheric coverage, compared to ratios in the mid-30s to mid-60s for circular orbits with global coverage. In general, if urgency is not the issue, a small number of orbital positions in high-altitude elliptical orbits (e.g., two per hemisphere in 24-hour-period orbits) might be preferable if a delay between weapon release and target impact of about 12 hours is tolerable. However, other things being equal, terrestrial basing is still the most economical for this class of weapon.

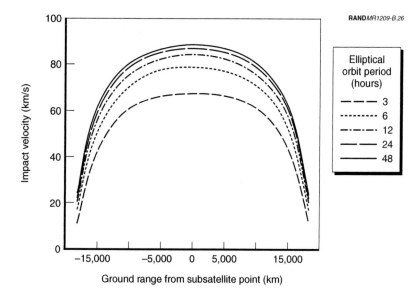

RAND*MR1209-B.26*

**Figure B.26—Impact Velocity for Minimum-Energy Deorbit
from Elliptical Orbit Apogee**

Terrestrial Basing

As noted earlier, President Eisenhower's advisors judged that earth is a better weapon carrier than a satellite. The graphs in Figures B.11 and B.24, which show the total Δv needed to base a weapon in orbit and deorbit it onto a target, included a box indicating the rough velocity range needed to deliver a weapon in a steep ICBM-like trajectory from the surface of earth. The details are in Figures B.31 and B.32.

Figure B.31 shows the burnout and impact velocities for ballistic trajectories constrained to a reentry angle of 60 degrees, the minimum for accuracy. The impact velocity assumes the same weapon β as in the earlier orbital basing figures. To measure the logistic effort for

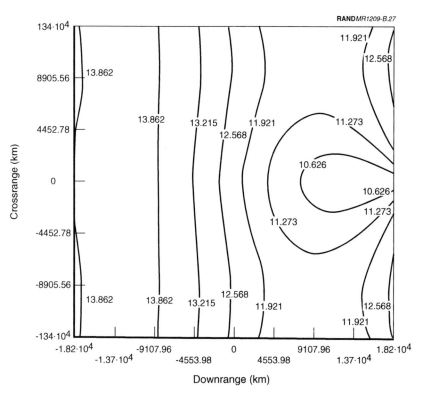

Figure B.27—Total Δv for 6-Hour Elliptical Orbit Apogee

transporting the weapon to target, compare the burnout velocity with the total Δv for the orbital cases.[14]

Figure B.32 shows the time of flight needed for the lofted ballistic missile trajectories. At longer ranges, a fractional orbit trajectory may be necessary to keep the time of flight reasonable. But if the weapon is based, for example, on a ship or submarine and if its range

---

[14]Both velocities are ideal in that they neglect gravity and atmosphere losses in reaching orbit or burnout, which is acceptable for comparing relative differences. To estimate the real velocities needed, include about 1 km/sec of loss for each.

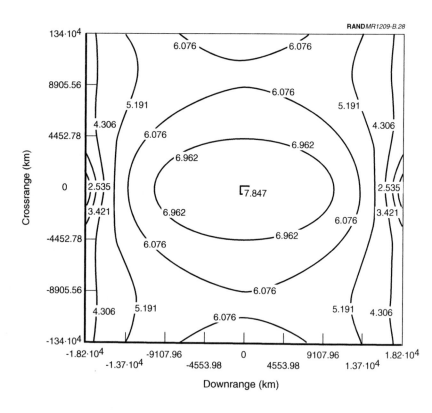

Figure B.28—Impact Velocity from 6-Hour Elliptical Orbit Apogee

from the target is suitable for a lofted ballistic trajectory with a reasonable time of flight, the ideal propulsion effort is only about 8 to 10 km/sec, compared to the 10 to 12 km/sec for elliptical orbit basing and the 12 to 15 km/sec for circular orbit.   Depending on the propulsion specifics and losses, these velocity requirements would translate into propulsion needs per weapon mass of about those listed in Table B.5.[15] Note that Scales (1999, pp. xvi, 88) stated that it took 40 tons of fuel to drop 1 ton of bombs during the Persian Gulf War.

_____

[15]These ratios are very rough magnitudes, useful only for relative comparison among general basing alternatives. Better estimates for absolute sizing would require detailed examination of staging, propellant performance, and inert (nonpropellant) weight budgets.

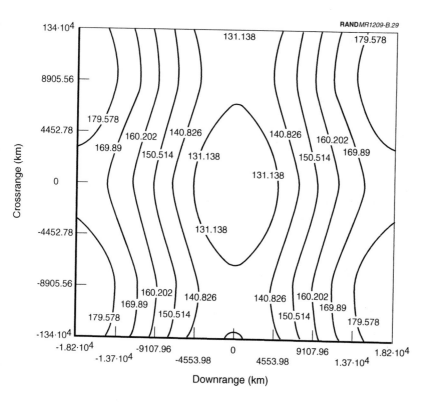

Figure B.29—Time of Flight from 6-Hour Elliptical Orbit Apogee

Another issue is the absentee ratio to achieve the desired degree of responsiveness for a given basing mode. As noted earlier, this ratio may range from 2 to over 60 for orbital basing. But propulsion mass is only one element of the logistic costs for delivering these weapons.

The logistic cost of acquiring and supporting terrestrial bases—particularly ships and submarines, which have their own absentee ratios set by endurance limits, transportation delay, and maintenance or refit time—may be higher than the propulsion cost for orbital basing. Also, terrestrial platforms have operational signatures similar to those normally associated with nuclear weapons; this could make such platforms unattractive for other kinds of weapons in a way that overshadows logistic cost issues.

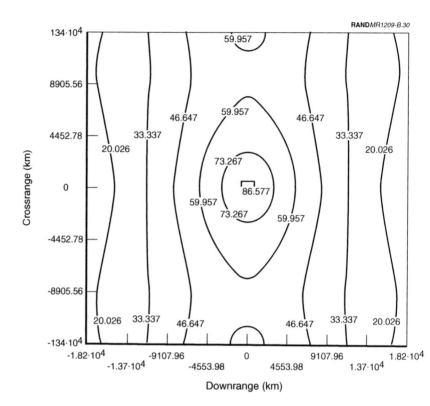

Figure B.30—Reentry Angle from 6-Hour Elliptical Orbit Apogee

Table B.4

Sample Elliptical Orbits

Orbit Period (hours)	Apogee height[a] (km)
3	7,964
6	20,370
12	40,060
24	71,330
48	121,000

[a]All perigee heights are 400 km.

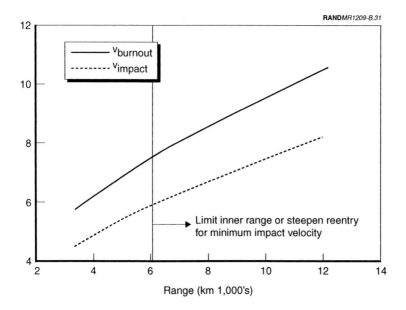

Figure B.31—Velocities for Ballistic Trajectory from Terrestrial Base with 60° Reentry Angle

Table B.5

Propulsion Requirements for Kinetic Energy Weapon

Trajectory	Propulsion Type	Launch-to-Payload Mass Ratio
Ballistic	Solid propellant (expendable)	~20–60
Ballistic	Liquid propellant (e.g. reusable)	~16–40
Elliptical orbit	Liquid propellant	~30–55
Circular orbit	Liquid propellant	~55–140

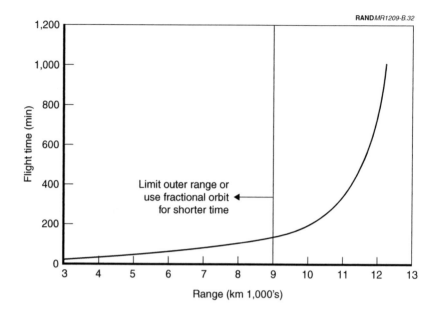

Figure B.32—Time of Flight for Ballistic Trajectory from
Terrestrial Base with 60° Reentry Angle

CONVENTIONAL WEAPONS

For space-basing conventional weapons, timely response and long
logistic reach still conflict, but the conflict is easier to resolve than it
was for kinetic-energy weapons. Figures B.19 and B.20 show this
conflict for a 8,000-km orbit. In Figure B.19, the area a weapon can
reach economically is on the right; in Figure B.20, the area a weapon
can reach in a short time is on the left. Constraining either parameter will mean compromising the other somewhere in the middle.
However, because a steep reentry angle and a high reentry velocity
are no longer constraints (or even desirable in this case), the base
orbit can be substantially lower, to provide greater responsiveness
without penalizing the footprint for the logistic effort.

Figures B.33 and B.34 show the corresponding contours of total effort
and reentry time for a 500-km orbit. The lower orbit allows a slightly

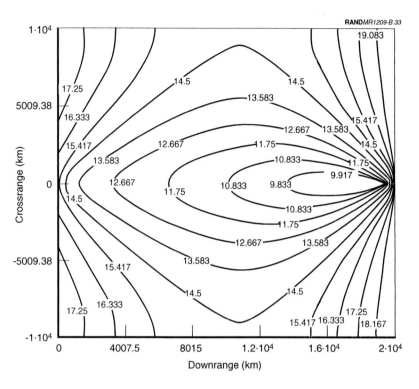

Figure B.33—Total Δv (km/s) for 500-km Circular Orbit

larger footprint for the same total effort, with reentry of the atmosphere within about 20 to 40 min, compared to 50 to 80 min at the higher altitude.[16] Also, since the time to complete an orbit at the lower orbit is one-third that of the higher orbit, the constellation of footprints can be less densely packed because the footprints move faster over earth's surface. For continuous, global access to targets, an absentee ratio of about 5 should be possible at 500 km with a responsiveness of about one-half hour from decision to destruction,

---

[16]However, the share of the total effort apportioned to deorbit (as opposed to launch) is greater at the lower altitude, so the magnitude of the observable deorbit rocket burn is correspondingly greater. In each case we could keep the flight times closer to the shorter end of the range of times available in close, using the excess propulsion available at the far end of the footprint to take a higher-energy, shorter time trajectory.

for total logistic effort of about the same order as for kinetic-energy weapons.

The comparison of terrestrial basing with orbital bases for this class of weapon parallels that for the kinetic-energy weapon. However, removing restrictions on the reentry angle and Δv changes the ranges and flight times of possible interest. Figure B.35 shows the equivalent of Figure B.32 for a relatively shallow 30-degree reentry angle (below the horizon), instead of the 60-degree reentry angle for kinetic-energy vehicles. For equivalent flight times and effort, standoff ranges of up to 20,000 km are possible with the shallower reentry, compared to the 9,000-km constraint for the steep reentry. ICBM trajectories would be more economical for this class of weapon

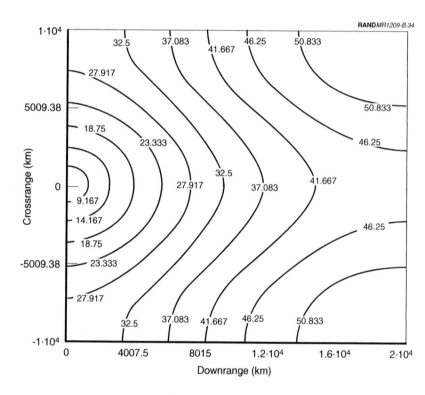

Figure B.34—Time of Flight to Reentry (min) for 500-km Circular Orbit, Minimum Energy Path

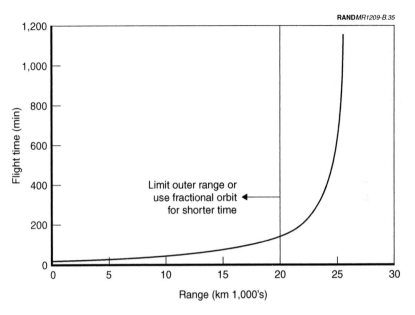

**Figure B.35—Ballistic Trajectory from Terrestrial Base with 30°
Reentry Angle—Time of Flight**

than space basing if confusion with nuclear-armed missiles can be
avoided. This might be possible if a vehicle is developed specifically
for the purpose, such as a reusable vehicle, or possibly with ICBMs
based in some verifiably distinctive mode.

Appendix C

NATURAL METEOROIDS AS WEAPONS

Chapter Three and Appendix B used the physics of meteoroids as a starting point for developing an understanding of kinetic-energy weapons delivered from space. The discussions examined idealized meteoroids at sizes having effects that would be of tactical interest in conventional warfare. The impressive effects on earth of past large meteoroids suggest the possibility that natural objects—earth-crossing asteroids—could be used as weapons on a scale more suitable for strategic deterrence, as are nuclear arsenals. Such notables as Carl Sagan, in discussing means of preventing catastrophic natural collisions, have expressed concern about the possibility of deliberately deflecting an asteroid toward earth as a weapon (Harris et al., 1994; Sagan, 1994; Sagan and Ostro, 1994).

For nations that already have nuclear arsenals, asteroid weapons might be of only academic interest. Depending on the relative difficulty of acquiring a nuclear arsenal or equivalent weapons of mass destruction, the idea might be of more practical interest to other nations. The decision process and motivations that might lead some nation to acquire such weapons were discussed in Chapter Six.

This appendix will review some of the practical issues in employing asteroids as weapons. As in Chapter Three, the critical military issues are the suitability of the effect and the logistics of causing it. The review here will discuss suitability briefly and logistics in more detail. Suitability is determined by the size of the effect desired, which depends on the size, velocity, and composition of the asteroid. Logistics is a question of timely availability of an asteroid and the effort needed to find and use one when desired.

WEAPON SUITABILITY

By the time very small meteoroids impact the ground, they have slowed to several hundred or a few thousand miles per hour. These meteoroids are too small for this discussion. Very large asteroids or comets penetrate the atmosphere as if it were not there and strike the ground with full force. At the larger end of this scale (diameter ≥1 km) are asteroids, whose effects are too great to be useful for strategic deterrence. Threats of a mass extinction event are not likely to be credible. At the lower end of the scale are meteoroids large enough to survive reentry to strike the ground; these represent the upper bound of interest for strategic deterrence. Asteroids that can survive to a low enough altitude to have blast effects represent the lower bound.

Intermediate-size asteroids explode in the atmosphere. The altitude at which such objects begin to explode is approximately determined by equating the crushing strength of the material to the local atmospheric density and the square of the instantaneous velocity. Asteroids have median entry speeds of 13 to 17 km/sec (Chyba et al., 1994). Iron asteroids that are only 10 m in diameter retain most of this speed even in the lower atmosphere. Small iron meteorites have crushing strengths of as much as 4,000 atmospheres. A statistical analysis of the weakening due to fractures would suggest slightly lower strengths for an object with a diameter of several meters to a few tens of meters (Lewis, 1997, p. 380), with fragmentation beginning at about 1 to 10 km. Substantial blast and heat effect could occur on the ground below if the fragmentation takes place near the lower limit of that range.

There were at least three demonstrations of the effects in the 20th century alone (ordered from largest to smallest):

* Tunguska, Siberia, June 30, 1908. An asteroid weighing about 100,000 tons exploded at an altitude of between 2.5 and 9 km, with a yield equivalent to 40 megatons of TNT (Vasilyev, 1996). The blast felled trees over 2,500 km² and burned 1,000 km². Had this explosion taken place over an urban area in Europe, it might have produced 500,000 human casualties (Gallant, 1993).

* Sikhote-Alin mountains, Kamchatka Peninsula, 1947. An asteroid estimated to have originally had a mass of less than 1,000

tons fragmented at an altitude of around 5 km. The burst was high but did produce some ground effects, and the explosive yield was close to that of the Hiroshima and Nagasaki atomic bombs. Over 30 tons of material have been recovered from this event (Vasilyev, 1996).

* The Amazon, August 18, 1930. This smaller but still impressive impact occurred in a remote region. This yield was about one-tenth that of Tunguska, and reports of the event have resurfaced only in recent years (Schaefer 1998).

Smaller asteroids produce no more damage than the psychological effect on the viewing population (although demonstrating the capability of delivering an asteroid to earth precisely and on schedule would have high deterrence value). On October 9, 1997, a fireball was observed from Santa Fe to El Paso, where it finally exploded at a height of 36 km and released energy estimated to be equivalent to about 500 tons of TNT (Schiff, 1997). Assuming a stone asteroid— since no meteorites were recovered—the diameter was estimated to be 2 m and the mass 20 tons. Similar events happen a few times each year. This one was notable because the meteoroid exploded high over a major population center.

Much-more-energetic events have occurred recently. What was reportedly the brightest fireball to be seen by a satellite resulted from a explosion on February 1, 1994, 20 km over a remote area of the western Pacific Ocean; the yield was estimated at 11 to 110 kilotons. The object responsible was probably a stony meteoroid with a diameter of 7 to 15 m (*Satellites Detect Record Meteor*, 1994). If the El Paso object had been this size, the ground effects would have been very minor, but the population of El Paso would have had much more to talk about.

In 1996, a large asteroid designated "1996 JA1" approached earth—453,000 km at closest. This is slightly more than the distance to the moon, but some asteroids have been observed passing within a fraction of the earth-moon distance. This particular asteroid is distinctive because it was observed only four days before its closest approach and is believed to have had a diameter over 100 m. The impact of such an object would produce a ground or near-ground explosion equivalent to a 100-megaton weapon.

In summary, the suitability of weapon effect depends on the combination of size and materials. Precise control of the effects in an impact area would be very challenging. An object large enough to cause a big explosion would generally have a high enough β to suffer only minor angular changes in its trajectory due to atmospheric effects. But even for such objects, precisely predicting the extent of destruction would require understanding their internal composition, including possible internal fracture statistics or heterogeneity, to predict the altitude of breakup and the extent of blast effects from the breakup. The breakup of the Brenham stony-iron meteorite, for example, produced some specimens that are essentially iron metal and others that are mixtures of iron and olivine, a variety of stone.

LOGISTICS

Availability

Two well known groups of asteroids—the Atens and the Apollos—currently cross earth's orbit, and each originates in the main asteroid belt between Jupiter and Mars. Astronomers have discovered 190 that are over 1 km in diameter and estimate that there are 900. In addition, the 1,500 Amor asteroids are believed to be very large near-earth objects that could pose significant future danger, having the potential for global destruction.

Among the smaller, potentially useful objects may be over 1 million asteroids over 30 m in diameter that cross the earth's orbit (Rabinowitz et al., 1994; Shoemaker et al., 1995). The objects among them that are important for this discussion have diameters ranging from a few tens of meters to a few hundred meters, depending on whether they are stone or iron and on the effect desired. The relevant questions here are

- Can we reasonably expect to find enough of them?
- Do they pass near enough to the earth to be deflected enough for accurate collisions with the earth?
- Can this be done quickly enough?
- Can we expect to find them whenever necessary?

The lower bound on the availability of likely candidates can be determined from the history of actual natural collisions. The upper bound will depend on the amount of effort and lead time that can be devoted to deflecting what would otherwise be near misses into precise impacts. The frequency with which earth-asteroid collisions occur without assistance has been estimated from satellite observations and from extrapolations by counting lunar craters (Morrison et al., 1994). Objects of the 10-m diameter class impact almost annually. Stone objects this small fragment too high up to be useful weapons. Iron meteorites are observed in 3.2 percent of all falls (Lewis, 1997, p. 323). It would therefore follow that a 10-m iron asteroid—a Sikhote-Alin class object—strikes land on average once per century or so and the ocean twice as often. Objects with diameters of 100 to a few hundred meters impact earth naturally with a frequency of about one in a few thousand years (Morrison et al., 1994). Iron objects produce craters like the Barringer crater in Arizona. Stony objects produce air bursts like the Tunguska event in Siberia.

Increasing the opportunities to employ one of these natural weapons requires increasing the range of near-misses to some maximum miss distance. As the area the maximum miss distance covers expands, the incidence of objects available to divert should increase in proportion to the increased cross-sectional area. For example, diverting asteroids that would otherwise miss earth by a distance as far as the average distance to the moon should multiply the incidence of "near-enough" misses by about 3,600. If it is possible to divert objects at such distances, suitable opportunities would be available as often as weeks or months apart, rather than years or centuries.

Effort

Diverting the course of an asteroid requires only a small Δv, if the deflection is done far enough in advance of earth impact. The displacement is proportional to both the lead time and Δv.[1] Done well

---

[1]Calculations of the Δv needed to *protect* the earth often assume that the asteroid is predicted to strike the earth and that the minimum deflection is about one earth radius. The assumed lead times are often very long, reducing Δv estimates to numbers much smaller than those assumed here for an asteroid used as a weapon. Deflecting an object toward earth requires a larger Δv if the miss is predicted to be close but by a

in advance, diverting an asteroid that would otherwise come no closer than midway between earth and moon requires imparting a Δv of at least several tens of meters per second to the asteroid. Deflecting an asteroid within days of its closest approach to earth would require a very large Δv, on the scale of kilometers per second. It is only possible to deflect an intermediate-size asteroid well in advance.

The precision of the angle and timing of entry into the atmosphere determine the degree of control over the location of the impact. Because the lead time for deflecting an asteroid is long, it is precise control of the velocity vector applied to the asteroid, not the time deflection begins, that is important. An error of only about 1 percent could alter the impact point by about 1,000 km.[2] In practice, ensuring damage to a particular large, soft earth target would mean controlling the asteroid's Δv to at least 1 part in 10,000. Reducing the target error to the range of kilometers would mean controlling the Δv to 1 part in 100,000, an accuracy comparable to that of simple ballistic missiles. The instantaneous position and velocity of the asteroid must be known during the deflection process and must continue to be monitored afterward for perturbations to the asteroid's trajectory. Radio astronomy provides the means of obtaining such precise position and velocity measurements: the differential, very-long-baseline interferometry used to navigate deep-space probes.[3] And, because of their large mass, these objects inherently have βs high enough to preserve accuracy through atmospheric entry. The principal uncertainty would be in the altitude of fragmentation for asteroids chosen to achieve blast, rather than impact, effects.

---

safe margin. Precise targeting would need to account for the enhancing effect of the earth's gravity well.

[2]Infrequent observations alone cannot provide sufficient trajectory precision for targeting. For example, a 1997 prediction claimed that a large Apollo asteroid, 1997 XF11, would approach earth on October 26, 2028, at a dangerous minimum miss distance of 28,500 km. Subsequent calculations using additional data revised the distance to 865,000 km. The width errors were, respectively, 2,550 km and 750 km. Even the improved error value would be inadequate if the goal were to manipulate a piece of this asteroid to impact on earth. Furthermore, the refined length uncertainty, at 174,000 km, was still large.

[3]The Deep Space Network's representative error budget for deep-space probe velocity measurements, under standard observing conditions, is about 0.1 mm/sec (Jet Propulsion Laboratory, 1997).

Other observers might eventually detect the changed trajectory and recognize the threat, perhaps using the same radio signals used for navigation. But what if the asteroid is not detected until the last part of its trajectory? In this case, the larger the object, the less chance even an advanced nation has of diverting it. Likewise, if the object is not already on course for impact, even the attacker can do little to correct the situation.

A nuclear weapon may be the only way to divert or fragment an asteroid of modest size in the days just before the expected impact— assuming one were available and ready to launch. Even then, the consequences would be uncertain, since this could just distribute the damage over a larger area, with higher-altitude bursts than the attacker intended. While this might be attractive for deflecting an asteroid *away* from earth on short notice, it would probably not have enough precision for deflecting an asteroid *toward* an earth target.[4] Given enough lead time, however, a number of other deflection methods are available.

The most straightforward nonnuclear approach is to attach a device to the asteroid to act as a mass launcher, using the asteroid's own material as propellant and the sun as a power source. Consider a device that could produce exit speeds of about 1 km/sec.[5] Deflecting an asteroid large enough to create effects comparable to those of the Sikhote-Alin event with a lead time before impact of less than a month would require ejecting at least several tens of tons of asteroid material. This could be done in one day if the continuous firing rate were 1 kg every few seconds. The launcher would be required to make tens of thousands of shots, and an error in a single shot would cause a noticeable target error. Prolonged firing would require a greater total number of shots, which would only partially reduce the firing rate.

Beginning the deflection months in advance would reduce the effort required and keep the firing rate low. Here, the Δv results from a

---

[4]In any case, a country that already had nuclear weapons would probably not need to use asteroids for deterrence.

[5]Sizing studies for lunar colonies have produced theoretical descriptions of such mass launchers. An early NASA study of space habitats describes mass drivers of larger capacity than our asteroid mover (Johnson, Holbrow, and editors, 1977).

large number of small nudges over a substantial period, so several times more effort would be needed than for a single large push (if that is even possible). The greater control that the prolonged multiple-shot process yields is, however, well worth the extra effort. Some of the key technical issues are development of a reliable mass launcher and the mining and preparation of asteroid material for use as propellant. Given enough lead time, the power needed for the mass launcher could also power the mining effort.

The amount of solar power needed for a mass launcher is large but not unthinkable for small asteroids. Firing 1 kg/sec at a speed of 1 km/sec requires 1 MW of power, assuming a mass launcher conversion efficiency of 50 percent.[6] A 2,500-m^2 solar array with 30-percent efficiency would be needed at a distance from the sun similar to that of the earth. Depending on the location of the asteroid at the time the maneuver begins, the distance might be as much as twice the earth-sun distance, which would require a solar array with four times the area.

Given a longer lead time than the postulated one month for moving something the size of the Sikhote-Alin object, the solar array could be smaller. Moving a massive Tunguska-like object would require two orders of magnitude (100 times) more energy. A reasonable level of effort for large objects like these could require a mass launcher to operate for months.[7] The equipment needed to convert an asteroid into a guided projectile would weigh tons, yet would have to be delivered at a velocity matching that of the asteroid. Depending on where delivery begins, this might be as prodigious a feat of propulsion as nudging the asteroid.[8]

---

[6]The average launcher power for the minimal iron asteroid mass that could penetrate close to ground with very high velocity would be an order of magnitude less. The approximation is for an object weighing on the order of 10,000 tons (i.e., explosive yield of about 200 kilotons).

[7]Even if it were possible to scale the mass launcher to eject material more rapidly from the larger objects, the power source would have to provide hundreds of megawatts—on the scale of a nuclear power plant.

[8]Another concept often considered for moving asteroids—the solar sail—requires very long lead times for a reasonable size sail and is therefore unattractive for diverting asteroids to weapon use, except perhaps to push one into a more convenient orbit years in advance.

Timing

The above discussion made it clear that the lead time for deciding to employ a specific asteroid as a deterrent will be at least months. Some preparations could be made years in advance that might eliminate some of the delay: surveying candidate asteroids, prepositioning propulsion capabilities, perhaps even modifying likely asteroid orbits to improve their availability. For use as a nuclear-equivalent deterrent, such preparations might even be necessary.

The history of nuclear deterrence would make such a lengthy response delay seem unreasonable. After all, in the time it would take to prepare and deliver an asteroid strike, an opponent might be able to force the asteroid wielder to relinquish its belated asteroid response. Thus, even with the best of preparations to shorten delays, the owner of an asteroid deterrent must convince potential opponents of the inevitability of its response. It helps that an asteroid on a collision path with the earth presents some physical basis for a perception of inexorability—particularly if the identity and location of the asteroid are not readily and quickly available to the defender. But the real difficulty would be human: conveying the credibility of a commitment to an irreversible, devastating response, even though a substantial delay that would allow time for second thoughts, recriminations, political changes, and opponent responses. In some cultures with longer memories and long-held grudges, a few months' commitment to purpose might be trivial.

Technology

Industrial-scale rocket propulsion is the fundamental technology necessary for turning asteroids into weapons. None of its elements are unknown. Proof of principle is well understood. Conceptual design studies are available in the literature on space and lunar colonization, although particular devices of the right size would need engineering development. Only the scale of the enterprise gives pause and invites comparison with World War II's Manhattan Project.

As the nation mobilized for war, total U.S. defense outlays went from about $2 billion a year to a peak of about $80 billion a year over five years (Clinton, 1997). The country spent about $2 billion in total (about $20 billion in 1996 dollars) to develop the scientific basis of atomic weapons and the industrial processes and infrastructure for extracting and refining the needed materials (Purcell, 1963, p. 13; JSC, 1998).[9] Because of the sense of urgency, the project pursued parallel development paths—four paths for materials extraction, two paths for weapon design—without waiting for success in prerequisite elements of the program before committing resources to dependent elements. Yet for all its unprecedented scale, extravagant urgency, and remarkable success, the Manhattan Project was relatively modest compared to what would be required for asteroid weapons.

Generating solar power in space for transmission to earth would provide a better reference point for our purposes. In 1977, the first proposals to develop a such a capability, with a capacity of 5 GW, estimated a cost of $102 billion (about $254 billion in 1999 dollars) (Landis, 1990). Later proposals tried to reduce the cost by using lunar material to produce the solar cells and other elements of the power infrastructure, which presumed a separate investment in lunar transportation and facilities (Landis, 1998). The transportation, space materials, and manufacturing technologies needed for that exercise are precisely those required to convert asteroids into suitable weapons and are of roughly the same scale.

Clearly, a "Manhattan Project" for an asteroid weapon would be large and difficult to conceal, except perhaps as an element of a larger, nominally civil, program that required a similar large-scale space infrastructure, such as a program for generating power economically in space or for extracting lunar materials for various large-scale activities in space.

ALTERNATIVES

Aside from the limited range of possible effects and the great uncertainty about the precision of an effect, one clear argument against asteroids as weapons is that smaller, cheaper means of acquiring an equivalent to a nuclear deterrent are available. The preceding com-

---

[9]When it was first decided to commit resources to industrial-scale production of atomic bomb materials, the estimate of future needs was only $400 million (Smyth, 1945, p. 115).

parison with the Manhattan Project highlights the fact that the infrastructure costs for asteroid weapons are at least an order of magnitude greater than the cost for developing and producing nuclear weapons.

Had it not been for the fortunate interruption of the Persian Gulf War, Iraq would have provided an example of the practicality of a covert, third-world "Manhattan Project." With that object lesson still fresh, the availability of nuclear materials and technology may have undergone enough scrutiny to make other alternatives attractive to those who would like to acquire a weapon of mass destruction. Unfortunately, chemical and biological weapons are much less expensive and much easier to proliferate than are nuclear weapons (OTA, 1993a; OTA, 1993b). While the alternatives may lack the impressive physical destruction of a nuclear or asteroid weapon, their potential for wholesale and indiscriminate lethality should make them reasonable substitutes for deterrence.

SUMMARY

With some patience, waiting perhaps a month or two, suitable asteroids could be routinely found that would produce weapon effects equivalent to nuclear weapons with yields ranging from tens of kilotons to many megatons. With some effort, they could be diverted to weapon using technology (and extensive supporting infrastructure) similar to that for exploiting lunar materials, generating solar power with satellites, or defending against asteroids. However, at best, it would take months after a decision to use one as a weapon to reach the desired conclusion. Because much cheaper, more responsive weapons of mass destruction are readily available, this one is likely to remain safely in the realm of science fiction.

BALLISTIC MISSILE DEFENSE COUNTERMEASURES

Chapter Five asserted that unsophisticated countermeasures could readily saturate terminal and midcourse missile defenses based in the continental United States. In discussing the urgency of boost-phase missile defenses, Chapter Three introduced the countermeasures. This appendix contains a thought-experiment to illustrate the possibility of an unconventional, unsophisticated countermeasure against terminal-area ballistic-missile defenses. The appendix also illustrates a possible unconventional, space-based deterrent weapon.

The straightforward approach to defeating midcourse and terminal missile defenses is to saturate them with multiple aim points. One way to saturate defenses during the midcourse portion of a missile's trajectory outside the atmosphere is to deploy relatively inexpensive, unsophisticated decoys (such as balloons or fragments of the booster) in large numbers and to alter the appearance of real targets to help confuse sensors trying to sort the real and false targets, for example, by deploying the real targets in what amounts to another decoy (APS, 1987; Lewis and Postol, 1997). By the time the decoys and a typical nuclear reentry vehicle reach the atmosphere, the lower ballistic coefficient of the decoys will cause them to fall behind and allow terminal-area defenses to concentrate on the reentry vehicles in the time remaining before the weapon detonates (Bethe, Boutwell, and Garwin, 1986, pp. 64–68; Flax, 1986, pp. 43–46; Garwin and Bethe, 1968). Because making a decoy's ballistic coefficient and other observable signatures match that of a reentry vehicle carrying a weapon is roughly equivalent to making another reentry vehicle, the conventional approach to defeating the remaining terminal-area defenses is normally not to saturate them with false targets but to try to outmaneuver them. This technique originally involved faster reentry (higher ballistic coefficients) and, as the technology evolved, maneuverable reentry vehicles. Alternatively, the attacker can saturate the terminal defenses with real targets.

Either of these two approaches, maneuvering or multiple reentry vehicles, requires some degree of technical sophistication and more resources than we might associate with an unsophisticated opponent. However, an unsophisticated opponent may not follow the same development paths the United States or the Soviet Union took in developing their own strategic deterrent arsenals.

Launching a nuclear weapon in a reentry vehicle on a ballistic missile is not the only way to pose an unacceptable threat to the United States. Other possible weapons of terror or deterrence (depending on perspective and purpose) include chemical and biological weapons, and these may be more readily available to what might be called rogue states. Their proliferation is more difficult to detect or interdict than nuclear weapons. Their development signatures are identical to those of pharmaceutical research and production. Chemical weapons and agricultural chemicals need the same production infrastructure. The infrastructure for producing biological weapons is practically undetectable. Among these "poor man's nuclear weapons," the spores of anthrax bacteria have been described vividly in the open literature and in official information (DoD, 1998a; DoD, 1998b; OTA, 1993a; OTA, 1993b; Taylor, 1996). A few kilograms of the spores delivered in an inhalable form can cause extremely large numbers of fatalities in areas of high population density. Against that kind of a target area with that kind of lethality, precision delivery is not required, just widespread dispersal and rough timing relative to time of day and weather.

Defending against the means of delivering chemical and biological weapons for terrorist purposes (suitcases, shipping containers, car bombs, subway releases) is generally the realm of police, customs, coast guard, and intelligence agencies, rather than of the military. Some opponents of missile defenses are quick to point these means of delivery out as evidence of the futility of military missile defenses. However, if the weapons are intended as a military deterrent, their utility would be better served by more visible delivery means, such as aircraft or missiles. These delivery platforms still provide the opportunity for effective, unsophisticated counters to terminal-area missile defenses.

With shorter-range missiles, the acknowledged approach for saturating terminal defenses is to fractionate a unitary warhead into multiple submunitions and deploy them early in the trajectory (Lewis and Postol, 1997, p. 62). Some might think this approach applies only to short-range, theater missiles because the submunitions would not survive the heat of reentry associated with longer-range missiles unless their reentry vehicles were of the expense and complexity suitable for a nuclear weapon. However, that assumes an opponent would adopt a design philosophy that mirrors historical practice for nuclear reentry vehicles. It might instead be more effective to follow early practices in returning biological samples (cosmonauts, astronauts, and chimpanzees) to earth from orbital velocities. Small, low-tech submunitions for ICBMs of this type could deliver useful quantities of anthrax spores effectively against sprawling urban and suburban targets. The key insight comes from Appendix B's discussion of meteoroid reentry; all that is needed is a suitably low ballistic coefficient for the reentry vehicle.

Envision a submunition reentry vehicle design employing a spherical shape, thin-shell aluminum structure with a diameter of a few tens of centimeters, roughly the size of a basketball or globe. The spherical shape requires no attitude control in deployment and can be fabricated with the same spin-forming machines or presses that make pots and pans. It might use phenolic ablative material on the exterior made from the same materials used for insulating handles on pots and pans, brake pads, and the like (Tipco, 1998). To further insulate the few kilograms of biological payload from heat, the interior might be filled with mineral-fiber insulation (Rolan, 1999) and/or a vacuum flask dewar (which could simply be a Thermos™ bottle) in the center containing the anthrax spores. With a ballistic coefficient on the order of a few hundred pascals, such a container should lose most of its velocity above 30 to 40 km altitude and undergo a peak acceleration of about 100 g's, with manageable heating.

For fusing, the vehicle might sense its deceleration profile (see the characteristic shape in Figure B.2) using solid-state accelerometers, such as those used to deploy safety devices in automobiles, and perhaps timers to ignite detonation cord, open the package, and disperse the spores near the desired altitude (Eagle Technology, 1999). The timing could be tailored for the atmospheric conditions in the desired target area at launch time, using current barometric pressure downloaded from the Internet (The Weather Channel, 1999). All the materials and knowledge required are readily available around the world without breaking the threshold of export controls on missile technology. In testing with more conventional reentry vehicles, these submunitions might look like decoys, and their intended purpose might not even be detected. A thin, midcourse, or terminal-area missile defense would not be much help against modest numbers of these weapons.

The alternative to midcourse and terminal area defenses for this kind of threat is a boost-phase defense.[1] Where it is possible (or economical) to station a ship, airplane, or land-based defensive platform with fast interceptors or directed-energy weapons close enough to the launch area, space-based defenses might not be needed. However, for such areas as the interior of Iran, China, or some states of the former Soviet Union, only space-based defenses could attempt a boost-phase defense.

---

[1]Aside from deterrence, which was ground-ruled out of the discussion by defining the threat as a rogue or undeterrable state and which may not be relevant to a small state trying to establish its own deterrent to U.S. operations it finds counter to its interests. If the state believes it can deter U.S. conventional forces with the credible threat of a limited use of its own weapon of mass destruction, it might believe the U.S. nuclear deterrent stalemated.

ABM Treaty, Agreed Statement D.

Abrams, Jim, "House Backs Missile Defense System, Sends Bill to Clinton," *Boston Globe*, May 21, 1999.

ACDA—*See* U.S. Arms Control and Disarmament Agency.

AFSPC—*See* Air Force Space Command.

AF/XPX—*See* U.S. Air Force, Strategic Planning Directorate.

Air Force Association, "Space Firsts," *Air Force Magazine*, August 1998.

Air Force Space Command, 1998 Goals, Mission, 1998. Online at http://www.spacecom.af.mil/hqafspc/index.htm as of August 2, 1999.

Agence France Press, "Ministry Spokesman Admits Phone Jamming in N. Caucus," FBIS AU2411101599, Paris, 1999.

Ahmedulla, Mohammed, "India Looks to Russia for Help with Nuclear Subs," *Defense Week*, August 7, 2000, p. 1.

American Physical Society, "Science and Technology of Directed Energy Weapons—Acquisition, Tracking, and Discrimination," *Reviw of Modern Physics*, Vol. 59, No. 3, 1987, pp. S145–S2168.

Asphaug, Erik, "The Small Planets," *Scientific American*, May 2000, p. 46.

AURA, *Kitt Peak National Observatory*. National Optical Astronomy Observatories, March 30, 1999. Online at http://www.noao.edu/kpno/kpno.html as of April 7, 1999.

Barela, Timothy, "Anti-Armor Einstein," *Airman*, September 1996.

Barensky, Stefan, "ISIR Newsline Digest 2.20: Business & Mergers," *International Space Industry Report (ISIR)*, May 18, 1999.

Baucom, Donald R, "Developing a Management Structure for the Strategic Defense Initiative," in Roger D. Launius, ed., *Organizing for the Use of Space: Historical Perspectives on a Persistent Issue*, 18. San Diego, Calif.: Univelt, 1995, pp. 187–215.

Bender, Bryan, "US Blueprint for Future Weapons Systems Is Outlined," *Jane's Defence Weekly*, May 26, 1999.

Bethe, Hans A., Jeffrey Boutwell, and Richard L. Garwin, "BMD Technologies and Concepts in the 1980s," in Franklin A. Long, Donald Hafner, and Jeffrey Boutwell, eds., *Weapons in Space*, New York: Norton, 1986, pp. 53–71.

Bjork, R. L., *Analysis of the Formation of Meteor Crater, Arizona: A Preliminary Report*. Santa Monica, Calif.: RAND, P-2370, 1961.

Brodie, Bernard, and Fawn Brodie, *From Crossbow to H-Bomb*, Rev. and enl. ed., Bloomington: Indiana University Press, 1973.

Carter, Ashton B., Congressional Office of Technology Assessment, *Directed Energy Missile Defense in Space*, background paper, Washington, D.C.: U.S. Government Printing Office, 1984.

Carter, Ashton B., David N. Schwartz, *Ballistic Missile Defense*. Washington, D.C.: Brookings Institution and Massachusetts Institute of Technology, 1984.

Chyba, et al., "Impact Delivery of Volatiles and Organic Molecules to Earth," in Tom Gehrels, ed., *Hazards Due to Comets & Asteroids*, Tucson, Arizona: University of Arizona Press, 1994, pp. 9–58.

CIA—*See* Central Intelligence Agency.

Central Intelligence Agency, *World Fact Book*, 1996. (The 2000 edition is online at http://www.theodora.com/wfb/ as of November 20, 2001.)

Clauser, F. H., D. Griggs, L. N. Ridenour, P. A. Lagerstrom, G. H. Peebles, W. B. Klemperer, J. F. Lipp, E. S. Rutowski, R. W. Krueger, G. Grimminger, H. Luskin, B. Baker, E. W. Bradshaw, E. Wheaton, W. H. Wampler, E. W. Graham, R. Shevell, C. V. Sturdevant, and D. D. Wall, *Preliminary Design of an Experimental World-Circling Spaceship*. Santa Monica, Calif.: RAND, SM-11827, 1946.

Clifford, Neil, and Bart DePontieu, *SeeSat-L Home Page*. SeeSat-L, 1994. Online at http://www2.satellite.eu.org/sat/seesat/seesat index.html as of April 7, 1999.

Clinton, William J., *Economic Report of the President, Figure B-78. Federal Receipts and Outlays, by Major Category, and Surplus or Deficit, Fiscal Years 1940–98*. 1997. Online at http://www.umsl. edu/services/govdocs/erp/1997/contents.htm#1 as of March 30, 1999.

Cohen, Avner, *Israel and the Bomb*, New York: Columbia University Press, 1998.

Cohen, William, *Space Policy*, Washington, D.C.: Department of Defense, Directive 3100.10, July 1999.

Committee on Space Debris, *Orbital Debris: A Technical Assessment*. Washington, D.C.: National Academy Press, 1995.

Cox, Christopher, *U.S. National Security and Military/Commercial Concerns with the People's Republic of China*. Washington, D.C.: U.S. House of Representatives, Select Committee on U.S. National Security and Military/Commercial Concerns with the People's Republic of China, 1999.

Davies, Merton E., and William R. Haris, *RAND's Role in the Evolution of Balloon and Satellite Observation Systems and Related U.S. Space Technology*, RAND R-3692-RC, 1988.

DeKok, Roger, and Bob Preston, "Acquisition of Space Power for the New Millennium," in Peter L. Hays, James M. Smith, Alan R. Van Tassel, and Guy M. Walsh, eds., *Spacepower for a New Millen-*

nium: Space and U.S. National Security, New York: McGraw-Hill, U.S. Air Force Academy, Institute for National Security Studies, 2000.

DoD—*See* U.S. Department of Defense.

Dodd, Robert T., *Thunderstones and Shooting Stars: The Meaning of Meteorites*, Cambridge, Mass.: Harvard University Press, 1986.

Drozdiak, William, "Commander of Air War Says Kosovo Victory Near," *Washington Post*, May 24, 1999, p. A01.

Durch, William J., *National Interests and the Military Use of Space*, Cambridge, Mass.: John F. Kennedy School of Government, Center for Science and International Affairs, Ballinger Pub. Co., 1984.

Eagle Technology, "Model 3265 DIP Package Accelerometer," Capetown, South Africa, 1999. Online at http://www.eagle.co.za/model3265.html as of January 15, 2001.

Eisenhower, Dwight D., *Waging Peace: The White House Years 1956–1961*. Vol. 2, 1st ed., Garden City, N.Y.: Doubleday, 1965.

Emme, Eugene M., *Aeronautics and Astronautics: An American Chronology of Science and Technology in the Exploration of Space*, NASA, 1961. Online at http://www.hq.nasa.gov/office/pao/History/timeline.html as of July 2, 1999.

Estes, Howell M., *USSPACECOM Long Range Plan*, Colorado Springs, Colo.: Headquarters, U.S. Command, 1998.

FitzGerald, Frances, *Way Out There in the Blue: Reagan, Star Wars and the End of the Cold War*, New York: Simon and Schuster, 2000.

FitzGerald, Mary C., *The New Revolution in Russian Military Affairs*. London: Royal United Services Institute for Defence Studies, Whitehall paper series, 26, 1994.

Flax, Alexander, "Ballistic Missile Defense: Concepts and History," in Franklin A. Long, Donald Hafner, and Jeffrey Boutwell, eds., *Weapons in Space*, New York: Norton, 1986.

Fogleman, Ronald R., and Sheila E. Widnall, *Global Engagement: A Vision for the 21st Century*. Washington, D.C.: USAF, 1997.

Friedman, George, and Meredith Friedman, *The Future of War: Power, Technology & American World Dominance in the 21st Century*, New York: St. Martin's Griffin, 1998.

Futrell, Robert Frank, *Ideas, Concepts, Doctrine: Basic Thinking in the United States Air Force, 1907–1960*. Vol. 1, 2nd ed., Maxwell AFB, Alabama: Air University Press, 1989.

Gallant, Roy A., *"The Sky Has Split Apart!" The Cosmic Mystery of the Century*, Southworth Planetarium, University of Southern Maine, 1993. Online at http://www.galisteo.com/tunguska/docs/splitsky. html as of March 26, 1999.

Garwin, Richard L., and Hans A. Bethe, "Anti-Ballistic Missile Systems," *Scientific American*, March 1968, pp. 21–30.

Gertz, Bill, "China Sees Bombing as Deliberate," *Washington Times*, May 24, 1999, p. 1.

Gray, Colin S., *American Military Space Policy: Information Systems, Weapon Systems, and Arms Control*, Cambridge, Mass.: Abt Books, 1982.

Green, Constance McLaughlin, and Milton Lomask, *Vanguard: A History*, Washington, D.C.: NASA, 1997.

GSFC—See NASA Goddard Space Flight Center.

NASA Goddard Space Flight Center, *NGST Observatory Designs Overview*, September 10, 1998. Online at http://ngst.gsfc.nasa. gov/Hardware/designs.html as of February 26, 1999.

Hall, Keith, "Remarks at the Naval Research Laboratory 75th Anniversary Event," Washington, D.C.: NRO, 1998.

Hamilton, Rosanna L., and Calvin J. Hamilton, *Terrestrial Impact Craters*, 1995. Online at http://spaceart.com/solar/eng/tercrate. htm as of January 6, 1999.

Harris, A. W., G. H. Canavan, C. Sagan, and S. Ostro, "The Deflection Dilemma: Use Versus Misuse of Technologies for Avoiding Interplanetary Collision Hazards," in T. Gehrels, ed., *Hazards Due to Comets and Asteroids*, Tucson: University of Arizona Press, 1994.

Hermann, Walter, and James S. Wilbeck, "Review of Hypervelocity Penetration Theories," in Charles E. Anderson and U.S. Defense Advanced Research Projects Agency, eds., *Hypervelocity Impact: Proceedings of the 1986 Symposium*, San Antonio, Texas, October 21–24, 1986, New York: Pergamon Press, 1987, pp. 307–322.

JCS—*See* Joint Chiefs of Staff.

Johnson, Dana J., "The Impact of International Law and Treaty Obligations on United States Military Activities in Space," *High Technology Law Journal*, 1987.

Johnson, Nicholas L., *Soviet Military Strategy in Space*, New York: Jane's, 1987.

Johnson, Nicholas L., "Preliminary Analysis of the Fragmentation of the Spot 1 Ariane Third Stage," in Joseph P. Loftus, ed., *Orbital Debris from Upper-Stage Breakup*, Washington, D.C.: American Institute of Aeronautics and Astronautics, 1989, pp. 41–100.

Johnson, R.D, and C. Holbrow, eds., *Space Settlements: A Design Study*, Palo Alto, Calif.: Stanford University and NASA Ames Research Center, 1975 Summer Faculty Fellowship Program in Engineering Systems Design, 1977.

Joint Chiefs of Staff, *Joint Doctrine Capstone and Keystone Primer*, Washington, D.C., July 15, 1997. Online at http://www.dtic.mil/doctrine/jel/new_pubs/primer.pdf as of May 12, 1999.

JPL—*See* National Aeronautics and Space Administration Jet Propulsion Laboratory.

JSC—*See* National Aeronautics and Space Administration Johnson Space Center.

"Just a Normal Town," *New Scientist*, July 1, 2000.

Katzaman, Jim, "'Stealth Works,' Says Wing Commander," *Air Force News*, 1999. Online at http://www.af.mil/news/May1999/n19990506_990888.html as of May 7, 1999.

Killian, James Rhyne, *Sputnik, Scientists, and Eisenhower: A Memoir of the First Special Assistant to the President for Science and Technoogy.* Cambridge, Mass.: MIT Press, 1977.

Landis, Geoffrey A., *Solar Power from the Moon: Materials Refining for Solar Array Production on the Moon.* The Artemis Society, July 25, 1998. Online at http://www.asi.org/adb/02/08/array-materials-refining.html as of March 29, 1999.

_____, *An Evolutionary Path to SPS*, Island One Society, 1990. Online at http://www.islandone.org/Settlements/EvolutionaryPathSPS.html as of march 30, 1999.

Leibovich, Mark, "A Dream Comes Back to Earth: Missteps, Shortfalls, Glitches Have Iridium Scaling Back Expectations for Its Satellite Phone Service," *Washington Post*, May 24, 1999, p. F12.

Lewis, George N. and Theodore A. Postol, "Future Challenges to Ballistic Missile Defense," *IEEE Spectrum*, September 1997, pp. 60–68.

Lewis, John S., *Physics and Chemistry of the Solar System*. Rev. ed. San Diego: Academic Press, 1997.

Loeb, Vernon, and Steven Mufson, "CIA Analyst Raised Alert on China's Embassy," *Washington Post*, June 24, 1999, p. A01.

Long, Franklin A., Donald Hafner, and Jeffrey Boutwell, *Weapons in Space*, 1st ed., New York: Norton, 1986.

Maberry, Mike, *Haleakala Observatories.* University of Hawaii, 1998. Online at http://www.ifa.hawaii.edu/haleakala/ as of April 7, 1999.

Morrison, David, et al., "The Impact Hazard," in Tom Gehrels, Mildred Shapley Matthews, and A. M. Schumann, eds., *Hazards Due to Comets and Asteroids,*, Tucson: University of Arizona Press, 1994, pp. 59–91.

National Aeronautics and Space Administration, Jet Propulsion Laboratory, *DSN Document 810-5, Module VLBI-10*, March 12, 1997. Online at http://deepspace.jpl.nasa.gov/dsndocs/810-5/vl10/vl10.html#Universal as of June 8, 2000.

National Aeronautics and Space Administration, Johnson Space Center, *Cost Models—GDP Deflator Inflation Index,* 1998. Online at http://www.jsc.nasa.gov/bu2/Inflation.html as of March 30, 1999.

National Security Council, Space Policy Subcommittee, *U.S. Policy on Outer Space,* Washington, D.C., NSC 5814, 1958.

Nitze, Paul H., *SDI and the ABM Treaty,* Washington, D.C.: Department of State, Bureau of Public Affairs, 1985.

NOAO. *National Solar Observatory, Sacramento Peak.*

Noordung, Hermann (Herman Potocnik), The Problem of Space Travel: The Rocket Motor [orig. *Das Problem der Befahrung des Weltraums*], Ernst Stuhlinger and J.D. Hunley, eds., with Jennifer Garland, Washington D.C.: National Aeronautics and Space Administration, NASA History Office, NASA SP4026, 1995.

Nye, Joseph S, James A. Schear, Ashton B. Carter, and Aspen Strategy Group (U.S.), *Seeking Stability in Space: Anti-Satellite Weapons and the Evolving Space Regime,* Lanham, Md.: Aspen Strategy Group and University Press of America, 1987.

O'Connell, Robert L., *Of Arms and Men: A History of War, Weapons, and Aggression,* New York: Oxford University Press, 1989.

Office of the Assistant Secretary of Defense (Public Affairs), "New National Space Policy Announced," Washington, D.C., 1996. Online at http://www.defenselink.mil/news/Sep1996/b091996_bt540-96.html as of _____.

OASD(PA)—*See* Office of the Assistant Secretary of Defense (Public Affairs).

OTA—*See* U.S. Congress, Office of Technology Assessment.

Office of the Under Secretary of Defense (Acquisition and Technology), *Defense Acquisition Deskbook,* Washington, D.C., June 1, 1999. Online at http://www.deskbook.osd.mil/ as of June 5, 1999.

Outer Space Treaty—*See* United Nations (1967).

Payne, Keith B. *Laser Weapons in Space: Policy and Doctrine,* Boulder, Colo.: Westview Press, 1983.

Peebles, Curtis. *The Corona project: America's First Spy Satellites.* Annapolis, Md.: Naval Institute Press, 1997.

Purcell, John Francis. *The Best-Kept Secret: The Story of the Atomic Bomb.* New York: Vanguard Press, 1963.

Rabinowitz, David, et al., "The Population of Earth-Crossing Asteroids," in Tom Gehrels, Mildred Shapley Matthews, and A. M. Schumann, eds., *Hazards Due to Comets and Asteroids,* Tucson: University of Arizona Press, 1994, pp. 285–306.

Raines, Frank, Bob Bell, and John Hamre, "The Line-Item Veto," press briefing, Washington, D.C.: The White House, October 14, 1997. Online at http://www.pub.whitehouse.gov/uri-res/I2R?urn: pdi://oma.eop.gov.us/1997/10/20/4.text.1 as of January 15, 2001.

Raymond, R. C. *The Low-Altitude Space Patrol: A Suggestion for Defense Against Long-Range Ballistic Missiles,* Santa Monica, Calif.: RAND, 1954, D-2090-PR.

Ricks, Thomas E, "For These B-2 Pilots, Bombs Away Means Really Far, Far Away," *Wall Street Journal,* April, 19, 1999, pp. A-1, A-10.

Rolan, "Aislantes Minerales," product description, Mexico: Rolan, 1999. Online at http://www.rolan.com/home.htm circa January 2001.

Rosolanka, James J., *The Defense Support Program (DSP), "28 Years of Service": A Pictorial Chronology 1970–1998,* El Segundo, Calif.: Space Based Infrared Systems System Program Office, 1999. Online at http://www.losangeles.af.mil/SMC/MT/DSP/HISTORY/ Dsppg01c.htm as of January 15, 1001.

Roy, Kenneth, "Ship Killers from Low Earth Orbit," *Naval Institute Proceedings,* October 1997, pp. 1–43.

SACRAMENTO PEAK. NOAO, 1999. Online at http://www.sunspot. noao.edu/INFO/INTRODUCTION/sacramento_peak.html as of April, 7, 1999.

Sagan, Carl, and Steven J. Ostro, "Dangers of Asteroid Deflection," *Nature,* 1994.

Sagan, Carl, "Long-Range Consequences of Interplanetary Collisions," *Issues in Science and Technology*, Vol. 10, Summer 1994, pp.
67–72.

"Satellites Detect Record Meteor," *Sky & Telescope*, June 1994, p. 11.

Scales, Robert H., *Future Warfare*, Carlisle Barracks, PA: U.S. Army
War College, 1999.

Schaefer, Bradley E., "Meteor that Changed the World," *Sky & Telescope*, December 1998.

Schelling, Thomas C., "The Military Use of Outer Space: Bombardment Satellites," in Joseph M. Goldsen, ed., *Outer Space in World
Politics*, New York: Praeger, 1963, pp. 97–113.

Schiff, Joel, "El Paso Fireball," *Meteorite!*, November 1997.

Shalikashvili, John M., *Joint Vision 2010*, Washington, D.C.: Joint
Chiefs of Staff, 1996.

Shoemaker, Eugene M., et al., *The Near Earth Object Survey Work-
group Report*. NASA Ames Research Center, 1995. Online at
http://impact.arc.nasa.gov/reports/neoreport/index.html as of
March 29, 1999.

Smyth, Henry De Wolf, *Atomic Energy for Military Purposes: The
Official Report on the Development of the Atomic Bomb Under the
Auspices of the United States Government, 1940–1945*, Princeton,
N.J.: Princeton University Press, 1945.

Space Based Infrared Systems Program Office, brochure on SBIRS-
Low, El Segundo, Calif., 2000. Online at http://www.losangeles.af.
mil/SMC/MT/BROCHURE/brocure.htm as of January 15, 2001.

Spacehab, *Products and Services*, Online at http://www.
spacehab.com/products/index.html as of June 24, 1999.

Space Transportation Association, *"Going Public": Moving Toward
the Development of a Large Space Tourism Business*, 1999. Online
at http://www.spacetourism.org/ as of June 24, 1999.

STA—*See* Space Transportation Association.

Stares, Paul B. *Space Weapons and US Strategy: Origins and Development*. London: Croom Helm, 1985.

Taylor, Robert, "All Fall Down: Bioterrorism Special Report," *New Scientist*, 1996.

Technological Capabilities Panel, *Meeting the Threat of Surprise Attack*, February 14, 1955.

The Weather Channel. *Current Conditions, Washington, D.C.* weather.com, daily, 1999. Online at http://www.weather.com/weather/us/zips/20005.html as of June 19, 1999.

Tipco, Inc., "Thermoset Moulding Powders," . India: Tipco Inc, 1998.

United Nations, *Treaty on Principles Governing the Activities of States in the Exploration and Use of Outer Space, Including the Moon and Other Celestial Bodies*, January 27, 1967.

University of California, Observatories, Lick Observatory. University of California, 1999. Online at http://www.ucolick.org/lickobs/index.html as of April, 7, 1999.

U.S. Air Force, Strategic Planning Directorate, *Futures Game '98 Final Report*, Washington, D.C., 1998.

U.S. Arms Control and Disarmament Agency, Arms Control and Disarmament Agreements, Texts and Histories of the Negotiations, Washington, D.C., 1990.

U.S. Congress, Office of Technology Assessment, *Ballistic Missile Defense Technologies*. Washington, D.C., 1985.

_____, *Proliferation of Weapons of Mass Destruction: Assessing the Risks*. Washington, D.C., OTA-ISC-559, 1993a.

_____, *Techologies Underlying Weapons of Mass Destruction*. Washinton, D.C., OTA-BP-ISC-115.U.S, 1993b.

U.S. Department of Defense, *Anthrax: Fact vs. Myth*. DefenseLink, 1998a. Online at http://www.defenselink.mil/specials/Anthrax/myth.htm as of March 16, 1999.

_____ "Information Paper—Anthrax as a Biological Warfare Agent," *DefenseLink,* June 10, 1998b. Online at http://www.defenselink. mil/other_info/agent.html as of March 16, 1999.

U.S. Department of State, *Comprehensive Test Ban Treaty,* 2000. Online at http://www.state.gov/www/global/arms/ctbtpage/ trty_pg.html as of May 17, 2000.

U.S. Department of State, Office of the Spokesman, Fact Sheet: Second Agreed Statement, September 26, 1997.

U.S. Department of State, *Comprehensive Test Ban Treaty,* 2000. O   n   l   i   n   e   a   t http://www.state.gov/www/global/arms/ctbtpage/trty_pg. html as of May 17, 2000.

U.S. Geological Survey, *Tungsten in September 1998.* 1998. Online at http://minerals.er.usgs.gov/minerals/pubs/commodity/tungsten /68000998.pdf as of January 6, 1999.

U.S. Senate Armed Services Committee, *National Defense Authorization Act for FY 2000, Section 911: Commission to Assess United States National Security Space Management and Organization,* 106th Congress, 1st Session. Online at http://web.lexis-nexis. com/ as of June 1, 1999.

USGS—*See* U.S. Geological Survey.

UCO—*See* University of California.

United Nations, "Convention on the Prohibition of Military or Any Other Hostile Use of Environmental Modification Techniques," Geneva, 1977.

United Nations, "Treaty on Principles Governing the Activities of States in the Exploration and Use of Outer Space, Including the Moon and Other Celestial Bodies," London, Moscow, and Washington, 1967.

Vasilyev, N. V., *The Tunguska Meteorite Problem Today,* Commission on Meteorites and Cosmic Dust, Tomsk, Russia: Siberian Branch of the Russian Academy of Sciences, Tomsk University, and Kharkov, Ukraine: Kharkov Mechnikov Institute for Microbiology and Immunology, July 15–17, 1996. Online at http://www.galisteo.com/tunguska/docs/tmpt.html as of March 26, 1999.

Velikhov, E. P., R. Z. Sagdeev, and Andre i Afanasevich Kokoshin. *Weaponry in Space: The Dilemma of Security*, Moscow: Mir Publishers, 1986.

Wainscoat, Richard, *Mauna Kea Observatories*, Unversity of Hawaii, 1997. Online at http://www.ifa.hawaii.edu/mko/ as of April, 7, 1999.

Wells, H. G., *The War of the Worlds*, New York: Bantam Press, 1988.

The White House, Office of Science and Technology Policy, National Science and Technology Council, *National Space Policy*, Washington, D.C., September 19, 1996. Online at http://www.whitehouse.gov/WH/EOP/OSTP/NSTC/html/pdd8.html as of January 15, 2001.

Wilkening, Dean, and Kenneth Watman, *Strategic Defenses and First Strike Stability*. Santa Monica, Calif.: RAND, R-3412-FF/RC, 1986.

Wilkening, Dean, *Ballistic-Missile Defence and Strategic Stability*, London: International Institute for Strategic Studies, Adelphi Papers, 2000.

Woolman, R. Dan, *In Search of Tungsten*, 1996. Online at http://www.in-search-of.com/frames/periodic/elements/74.html as of January 6, 1999.

Wynn, Jeffrey C., and Eugene M. Shoemaker "The Day the Sands Caught Fire," *Scientific American*, November 1998. Online at http://www.sciam.com/1998/1198issue/1198wynn.html.